IN SEARCH OF SAFETY

Voices of Refugees

IN SEARCH OF SAFETY

Voices of Refugees

written & photographed by SUSAN KUKLIN

CANDLEWICK PRESS

First edition 2020

Library of Congress Catalog Card Number pending
ISBN 978-0-7636-7960-6

20 21 22 23 24 25 LGO 10 9 8 7 6 5 4 3 2 1

Printed in Vicenza, Italy

This book was typeset in Chaparral Pro.

Candlewick Press
99 Dover Street
Somerville, Massachusetts 02144

visit us at www.candlewick.com

For Mom and Pop

and

those still waiting

CONTENTS

PART IV: SURVIVE

Shireen | COUNTRY OF ORIGIN: Northern Iraq | ETHNIC GROUP: Yazidi

PART V: HOME

Dieudonné | COUNTRY OF ORIGIN: Burundi | ETHNIC GROUP: Hutu and Tutsi

PART VI: NOTES AND RESOURCES

Nebraska

WELCOME TO NEBRASKA, WELCOME HOME

Refugees are people who are forced to leave their country because they are being persecuted. From 1980 to 2018, the number of refugees resettled in the United States each year was between 50,000 and 100,000 people. In 2019, that number dropped to 30,000 people, and in 2020 it dropped again to 18,000. Many of them are from Southeast Asia, the former Soviet Union, Bosnia, the Middle East, and Africa. Some have resettled in the Midwest because housing there is reasonably priced and jobs are relatively plentiful. The five refugees featured in *In Search of Safety* are from Afghanistan, Myanmar, South Sudan, Iraq, and Burundi. One refugee had been a translator for the U.S. military. Another recently escaped the horrors of captivity by fundamentalist militants. And three spent years in refugee camps, growing up in countries other than their homeland. They all survived wars. They all were carefully screened by several security organizations, such as the United Nations High Commissioner for Refugees, the United States State Department, and the United States Department of Homeland Security. They have all been resettled in the state of Nebraska, where they have been warmly welcomed. This book tells their stories.

Lutheran Family Services is one of many nongovernmental organizations (NGOs) around the United States that arrange the resettlement of refugees. They organize volunteers to set up homes for newly arrived persons or families. In each case, an American individual or family acts as a sponsor. They help the new immigrants find jobs, shop, learn English (if necessary), arrange for the children's schooling, set up doctor's appointments, and do whatever else is needed to acclimate the new arrivals to American culture. I am grateful to them for their support with this project and for their dedication to the refugees who come seeking safety and shelter.

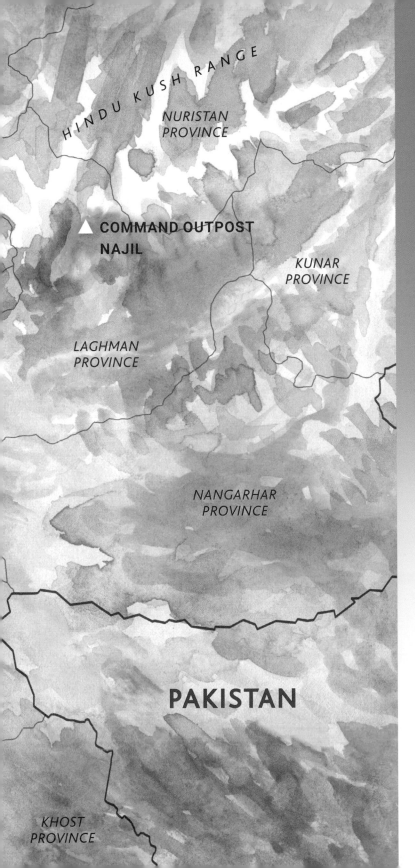

HINDU KUSH RANGE

NURISTAN PROVINCE

△ COMMAND OUTPOST NAJIL

KUNAR PROVINCE

LAGHMAN PROVINCE

NANGARHAR PROVINCE

PAKISTAN

KHOST PROVINCE

PART I
ARRIVE

Fraidoon

COUNTRY OF ORIGIN:
Afghanistan

ETHNIC GROUP:
Tajik

Fraidoon

1
The First Day of My Life

Fraidoon and his daughter, Leema, arrive in Nebraska on July 16, 2017, from Kabul, Afghanistan.

Fraidoon's wife, Homa, is holding Leema. Fraidoon and their son, Fardin, look toward the volunteers.

Tears of joy mix with billowing laughter. The volunteers are here to welcome their new neighbors who have just arrived from Afghanistan. Fraidoon and his family are refugees.

The volunteers had one week's notice to put an entire household together. They did it.

From 2004 until 2017, Fraidoon—his American military
buddies call him Fred—participated in more than five
hundred combat missions, a hundred of which were
under heavy fire. Retired FBI agent Dave Lemoine
says that in Afghanistan, Fraidoon saved hundreds of
American lives.

Fraidoon's work with the Americans left him with two choices: stay in Afghanistan and risk being killed, or move to the United States and live. The location of the town where the family lives cannot be revealed, because two fatwas against his life are still in effect. A fatwa is an Islamic legal pronouncement. In recent times, the word has been widely used to refer to a death sentence.

Afghani interpreters who are already living in the States greet the family with home-made Afghani foods and more flowers.

The family's mentors, Shane, Krynn, Max, and Mason Pekny, welcome them into their new home. In Fraidoon's case, he is self-sufficient because he speaks excellent English and has many military friends living here. This is not typical of most refugees.

"Gimme five."

"I didn't think it would be this nice. I wasn't expecting much. Trust me.

I wasn't expecting much at all."

The kitchen is stocked with halal food, in keeping with Muslim dietary law.

Lacey, the director of advancement for community services at the Lutheran Family Services of Nebraska, opens the children's new bedroom closet, chock-full of clothes and toys. Fardin goes for the toys.

No English necessary

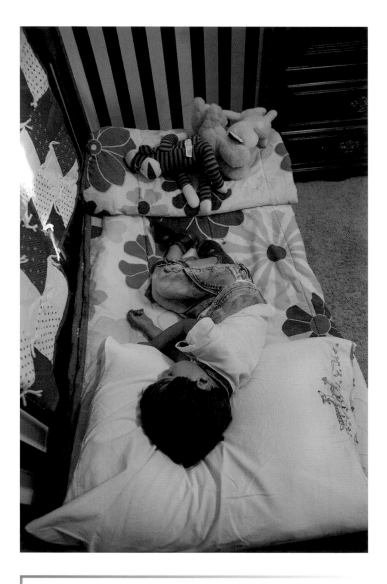

Leema slept through much of the arrival. She may not even know that she's now in her very own new bed.

2
Fraidoon

From 1984, when I was born, until July 16, 2017, when I arrived in the United States, I never lived in a place where there was no war. The year I was born, the Russians had been fighting in my country for five years. My father was a battalion commander in the Afghan National Army. The Afghan National Army was supported by the Soviet Union. They were fighting the Mujahideen, about fifteen separate guerrilla military parties, who were backed by Western countries, especially the United States. The Mujahideen did not like the fact that my father joined the Afghan National Army. For revenge, they killed his father, my grandfather. Yeah. They killed him, just because my father chose to serve his country.

In 1989, when the Russians left my country, my father thought the fighting was over. For this reason, he resigned from the military. He opened his own shop, a general store. But no, the fighting was not over. Civil war began when the fifteen Mujahideen parties fought each other for power. Many people were killed; many cities were destroyed. We thought that the fighting would never be over. We thought that we would never have peace in my country. We lost hope.

Seven years later, in 1996, when I was twelve, another group of fighters showed up. They called themselves Taliban. They were against the Mujahideen. They were against the Afghan army. They were against the government. They were against everybody.

The Taliban were a mix of mostly Pashtun Afghans, Pakistanis, Chechens, and Arabs. First they took over Kandahar Province, in the south, and from there they moved throughout the country. Osama bin Laden, the leader of Al-Qaeda, joined up with the Taliban as well.

The United States had given my country Stinger antiaircraft missiles to fight the Russians. When the Taliban took over, Pakistani militia, "advisers," collected the military equipment and took it to their country. But they left enough equipment for the Taliban to destroy my country, to destroy our national heritage. Once the Taliban took over, we began to miss the Mujahideen. The Mujahideen changed from bad people who fight to good people who help.

I was fourteen years old when the Taliban reached my city. We lived in the middle of Kabul. Kabul was usually a safer place than the rest of the provinces. But the morning the Taliban took over Kabul, we heard big fighting all around the city. My family had to decide what to do next. My dad didn't want to leave. He said, "We don't want to go to Iran or Pakistan. We are from Afghanistan. This is our country. This is our homeland, so we will not leave. If we are dying, we're going to die here." See, if you leave, it's a shame on you because people will think you didn't want to defend your country. For this reason, we thought we would stay forever.

The Taliban said that they would bring us peace. *Talib* is the Arabic word for "student." [*Taliban* is the plural.] A *talib* is a student of a religious school, what we call a *madrasa*. Some people thought they might be real *taliban,* real students of the *madrasa,* because they knew a lot of good things about Islam: religion, humanity, respect. We thought that they might do good things for the people. But we soon learned that these *taliban* were not students of Islam. I'm sure they were not able to read or pray like true religious Muslims do. Their top leaders told them to do something, and like sheep they did whatever they heard from their leaders.

We were told that the Taliban collected students from religious schools and sent them to fight jihad, to fight for human rights. This was completely wrong. This was not true. They never fought for the people; they never fought for the country. They were fighting for their own benefit. They were trying to cheat the people. We learned this in a matter of days.

We walked around the city, trying to find out what kind of people are these Taliban. We saw maybe two, three, hundred military vehicles with heavy equipment. The Taliban were walking around with machine guns and military equipment, but they didn't have uniforms. They never held up the flag of Afghanistan; they never wore a patch on their arm so that we knew where they were from. They were just a bunch of dirty people. Full of mud. We call what they wore man jammies, big, wide pants. They also wore turbans and had long beards.

At least the Mujahideen wore regular pants and uniforms. They were clean. The Taliban were a completely dirty and nasty people. They didn't know anything about respect for humans — not for kids, not for females. Nothing. Very quickly the Taliban's faces completely changed. They went from being humans to being animals. They got wild. And they started killing people. They didn't want to talk with us. They wanted to kill us. These people were mostly Pashtuns from the southern provinces, who, in one hour, completely changed our lives in Kabul.

Kabul had two TV stations. The stations broadcast music, news, cartoons for the kids, and other programs. After a few nights, the Taliban announced, "We're going to close the TV stations." They said that we cannot play our music anymore. They played their own music, which had no meaning for anybody. Their songs were not our songs. Their music was even in a different language, Pashto.

We're Tajik. We speak Dari at home. Pashto became the second language for my family.

The Taliban said that kids could not see cartoons anymore. They said that these things are illegal in Islam, and we were not allowed to watch them. Islam does not say that. I'm Muslim. I know that this is completely wrong.

They asked everybody to get ready for jihad. "What jihad?" we asked.

"It was time to kill the enemy," they said. The enemy was the Northern Alliance, one of the Mujahideen parties.

At this time, I was in the eighth grade. I remember my teacher telling us, "From now on, do not wear white socks. The Taliban flag is white. If you wear white socks, this means you disrespect their flag, and they're going to beat you up. Tell your mom and sister not to wear pants or anything white." All women had to cover their face. No women were allowed outside the house without a male family member accompanying them. A widow could not go out to shop for food for herself. What was she to do? Starve because she couldn't shop for food? Females were no longer allowed to go to school.

Before the Taliban, women had jobs just like men. They were in the army; they were lawyers and doctors and teachers, even bus drivers. The Taliban would no longer let the women work. They said that we don't need female doctors anymore. Someone told them, "If your wife is pregnant, you need a female doctor." So they let the female doctors stay in the hospital. But they did not let females teach, become pilots, or work in any Afghani organizations. Suddenly my sisters and my mother had to stay home. They couldn't do anything.

One of our favorite sports in Afghanistan is football [soccer]. The Taliban said, "No, you're not allowed." Why? "Because it's against Islam. The ball you're kicking represents the head of our prophet. Long, long ago, infidels fought with the Muslim people. They cut off Muslim leaders' heads and played with them as you would a ball. This means if you play with a ball, you're not a Muslim, because you're playing with the head of that prophet." This is completely wrong. They just made up some story for their own benefit. They turned our football stadium into a slaughterhouse.

Okay, we're not playing football. We're not going to let our mom and sisters go outside. We're not watching TV anymore. We will live in a dark age of fear, and it's going to be forever.

Then they said, "You guys are not allowed to play cards. It's gambling." I played cards with my dad all the time. I played with my sisters all the time. Our favorite games were King and Thief. We had nothing else to do. My dad was either at his shop or at home. I was half day at school.

Once we couldn't play cards, we secretly bought a TV and a VCR. We hid it somewhere in our house. When it was dark, we'd cover all the windows with cloth, take out the TV, and watch a movie. We didn't let anybody but the family watch. We were afraid that if our neighbors knew that we had a TV, they might tell the Taliban. Some people did tell the Taliban about their neighbors. "This house has cards." "That house has a TV." The Taliban would come into the house and break the TV. Then they would put the TV box over the person's head and a cord around his neck. They would walk him around the city like a dog on a leash. The man had to shout to the onlookers: "I'm sorry. I'm so sorry. I was watching TV, and the Taliban catch me. If you do like me, you will get punished like I did."

But then the Taliban made a mistake. They never told us that we could not learn English. Private English courses were given after school, and because I had nothing to do, I studied English. My regular school classes were from 6:30 a.m. to noon, and my English class was from 3:00 to 5:00 p.m., every day but Friday.

Then the Taliban did something that most people liked. They said that no one could steal things from somebody else's house. "If we catch that person, we will punish him severely. If you steal once, we will put you in jail and beat you up. If you steal a second time, we will cut off your left hand. If you steal a third time, we will cut off your right leg."

Back when my dad was a battalion commander in the Afghan National Army, the government sent him to Russia for more training and he learned the language. When the Taliban took over, they damaged the Russian military equipment and needed someone who knew how to fix it. Someone said, "That guy over there, he reads and speaks Russian. He knows a lot about the tanks." My father refused to help them.

After a few years — I don't remember the specific date — the Taliban attacked our house in the middle of the night and took my father away from us. My mother was pregnant at that time. My mom was so upset, she got sick, and we took her to the hospital. Some of our relatives went with us because my father was not home to take care of her. She gave birth to a boy. We brought him home the next morning. (Today, my brother is in his second year in college.)

I was still in school, but I tried to keep my dad's shop open, but it was too difficult. I sold the shop to a man who till this day has not given us all the money. I was a little kid. I didn't know how to get the money from the people who bought the shop. My mom didn't pay attention to such things. She said, "I don't care about the money. I just need everyone to be alive." We were in a very bad situation. My uncle stepped in and supported our family.

About two months after my father's abduction, my sister, who was twelve or thirteen, was looking out the window. A taxi stopped in front of our house. A man who looked a little bit like my father got out. My sister did not recognize this man. My father was a big guy, but the man who got out from the taxi was a skinny guy. "Hey, Mom," my sister said, "I see a guy outside our house. He looks a little like Father."

"Your father's gone," my mother told her. "He's not coming back, because they kidnapped him." We had had no news of my father's whereabouts. Finally my older sister, who was sixteen, looked outside. She screamed, "Oh, that's my father!" There was a great excitement.

Our father looked completely different. He was so skinny because they didn't give him food. They punished him a lot. They beat him. They kept him in a cell — all this because he would not fix their Russian equipment.

My father later told us that one of the top commanders of the Taliban picked up his weapon, put it to his head, and said, "I'm going to kill you right now. You have to fix my equipment."

My father would not back down. "No. I can't, because I don't know how to do it. I resigned from my job long time ago. I forgot everything." They didn't believe him and put him in jail.

One day, the Taliban and prisoners were eating lunch. My father asked a Taliban guard to relieve him from lunch for prayer time. Being Muslim, he prays five times a day. The guard said, "Okay. Go pray and then come back to the jail."

My father actually told him, "I'm not coming back. I'm running away." The Taliban laughed and said, "He's lying. He has nowhere to run."

As soon as my father was outside and alone, he climbed over the wall and stopped a taxi. He told his story to the taxi driver. "I'm going to help you," the driver said. "I'll take you away from here." The driver would not charge him any money, which was a good thing, because he had no money.

I don't know where the taxi driver dropped him off. I only know it was far away from the Taliban prison, and far away from us. He walked for five or six days from that location to home. He had no money, no friends, no family, no car, nothing. Some villagers gave him food and water as he walked from village to village. Once he reached Kabul, a taxi brought him home. We paid the driver.

We did not tell anyone that my father was home. Whenever someone asked, we said that we didn't know where he was. Some Taliban came to our house and asked, "Where's your father?" We said, "You took our father." Every day someone came to our house and asked for my father. "You took him. We don't know where our father is." We didn't even let our relatives know where he was. We didn't hide him in our house, because we knew that he would get caught there. We sent him to our best friend's house. A month later, the entire family moved to a new location.

SEPTEMBER 9, 2001

Before 9/11, there was 9/9. Two Arab "reporters" who worked for Al-Qaeda came to Afghanistan to talk with the top Mujahideen Northern Alliance leader, Ahmed Shah Massoud. They had a bomb hidden in their camera. As soon as they started to interview him, they blew up the bomb and killed Massoud. I liked Massoud. He was a great guy. The Americans liked him too. That killing shocked the world. It was the first suicide attack in Afghanistan.

Two days later, we heard that Al-Qaeda hit the World Trade Center in New York with airplanes. Al-Qaeda was working with the Taliban. A lot of innocent people were killed for no reason. Everybody was shocked.

When we heard that the United States was going to help the Northern Alliance fight against the Taliban, we worried that maybe the United States will bomb everywhere in the country. Maybe they will kill us as well.

The United States started bombing Kabul, not the whole city, just specific places where the Taliban lived. A small group of American Special Forces was already here, working with the Northern Alliance. Afghans told the Americans where to drop the bombs. One bomb missed and hit in the middle of someone's house. Seventeen innocent people were killed. The rest of the bombs hit their targets.

Once the U.S. dropped bombs on the Taliban, we thought we would soon be free. That's when my father came out from hiding. Yeah. We went back to our own neighborhood. People asked, "Where have you been?" My father told them what had happened to him.

A few days later, one of our relatives was delivering wheat from Mazar-e Sharif to Kabul in a jingle truck. A jingle truck is a big decorated truck. He knocked on our door, and my dad answered. "What's going on?"

"I saw Mujahideen fighters just behind the mountains, maybe five kilometers from Kabul City. They're going to capture Kabul tonight."

We were like, "No way."

"Yes, just remember this."

The next morning when we woke up, Kabul was completely changed. Kabul was taken over by Mujahideen and Northern Alliance fighters. And the streets were filled with dead Taliban bodies. Every street we walked, we saw ten, fifteen, twenty, dead Taliban. One lady — I believe she works for the U.N. now — took off her burka and burned it in the middle of a street. She was the first of many women to do this.

The dead Taliban were not buried like Muslims are supposed to be buried. No graves. No. No. No. No. They were thrown in a valley and left to rot. There was that much hate.

The people of Kabul completely changed. When the Taliban were in power, males were not allowed to shave. All the men shaved. They put on suits. They walked like kings. Oh, that was the greatest time. We had good times those early days because we thought we would have peace and peace and peace. The Taliban had run away. Al-Qaeda had run away. The Americans were here. We had no more concerns. Most people were happy that the Americans stayed here. We said, "Oh, they're going to bring everything for us."

The U.S. troops cleared most of the big cities of Taliban. Most Taliban went to Pakistan, but some small groups stayed in villages to fight against the U.S. troops and the Afghan National Army.

"WHO WANTS TO BE A LINGUIST?"

In 2003, I graduated high school. My father encouraged me to join the Afghan military, become a soldier, and do something to serve my country. I heard that the United

States Army in Bagram [an American air force base] was hiring linguists who speak English. I thought to myself, that's a great job. I could serve my country from the other side. I could help another country who is helping my country.

One of my friends, a classmate, and I went to the Bagram Airfield gate and talked to the American soldiers. That was the first time I had ever spoken to an American soldier. I asked him if they were hiring linguists. He said, "Yes. There's a company called Titan hiring people."

I waited, along with maybe fifty other people, at the main gate of the airfield. They opened the gate and asked, "Who wants to be a linguist?" Everybody raised their hand. They asked us who spoke Dari, English, and Pashto? The Americans were hiring Pashto translators because most Taliban are Pashtun. They were hiring us to talk with the villagers who only spoke Pashto. "Do you speak Pashto?"

"Yes, I do."

They gave me an English exam, a polygraph test, and a medical exam. That was a Thursday. They said, "Come back on Monday and we will give you the result of the tests."

I went back on Monday. "You passed." They made a badge for me and took me inside to meet my boss, Barbara. Barbara was from the USA, a good lady, a really good lady. She said, "We would like you to work here, while the other guys go on missions outside Kabul."

I'm not the kind of person who likes to sit behind a desk. I wanted to be part of the military. "No," I told her, "I would like to work outside. Let those other guys work inside." If you are part of the military, if you are on the first line of the war, you get to fight against terrorism. I told her, "Bagram is a safe place, a forty-five-minute drive to my home. I would like to go to the first line of the war."

"Okay, get your stuff together and come back."

I went home, but really I had nothing much to pack. A week earlier, I had graduated from high school. I was planning to go to college. Instead, when I passed the English exam, I joined the military. I never went to college.

My family had known nothing about this. I sat down with my mom and dad, my sister and brothers, and said, "I'm going."

"Going where?"

"I'm going to one of the provinces where security is not good."

"Who are you?" my dad asked. "Who do you work for?"

"I am a linguist."

"Really?" my dad said. "Did you pass a test?"

"Yeah, this is my badge, and I'm going on a mission tonight."

Most of my family was happy. My dad had been in the army and knew what was going to happen. My mom was kind of upset because this would be the first time I would be away from her. She was, like, "Oh you might be . . . might . . . something might happen to you." My dad interrupted: "The soldiers come all the way from United States to bring peace and prosperity to our country. Let him go help."

Being a Muslim person, I respect my family, especially my mom and my dad. We Muslims believe that if you do good things for your mom and dad, and they pray for you, you'll be alive forever. No one can kill you.

My mom and dad prayed for me while I picked out some clothes and put them in a bag. On April 4, 2004, at nine o'clock at night, I went back to Bagram Airfield to translate for the Americans.

3
Fred

As soon as I arrived at Bagram, I was given some uniforms, a sleeping bag, and shower stuff, everything. Until that step, I wasn't scared. Now that it was about to start, I got scared.

At one o'clock in the morning, they woke me up, put me in a car, took me to a helicopter, and flew me south, to Ghazni Province. Ghazni is one of the biggest provinces in Afghanistan. The Taliban were there, in the mountains, away from the city. As I speak about this, it is still unsafe.

Two hours later, we landed inside a PRT [Provincial Reconstruction Team] run by U.S. military forces. The PRT was doing construction projects. Next to them was a large military base for fighting against terrorism.

Later that morning, I met the American soldiers. They had big helmets, body armor, and guns. I didn't know what to say to them because I never knew anybody from the United States, civilians or military. I was younger than they were, and I wondered, like, hmm, what's going to happen now?

Three days later, for some reason, they selected me to work for the THT [Technical Human Team]. The THT was an investigating team that did top-secret work. When local spies brought information to the soldiers, my job was to translate what they said. Mostly I translated phone conversations. The callers gave us important information that led to finding caches of weapons and enemy activity.

The American soldiers and I became good friends. They called me Fred. We went on missions together. We ate in the chow hall together. We shared the same food and bottled water. It was like we had been friends for years.

I learned that the Americans were completely like us. Maybe we speak a different language, but we are the same. We had one aim: to fight against terrorism.

I worked with the soldiers for forty-five days, then went home for twenty days. When I went back to Ghazni, I was assigned to the battalion commander. I have no idea why they selected me. I was, like, hmm, he's a high-ranking person. He will be talking with very high-ranking people all the time. How can I work for him?

The battalion commander was a lieutenant colonel from 116th Virginia National Guard. Working for the battalion commander was hard, because once a week I had to go on TV and translate into Pashto what the commander said in English. Whoever saw me on TV, both citizens and terrorists, knew that I was working for the Americans. At the time, I didn't pay attention to it.

"WE THOUGHT WE WERE SAFE"

I worked for the lieutenant colonel for one year. When he and his battalion left, another group showed up. Then another group. I kept talking, talking, talking, learning a lot of things from the different units. I moved from one location to another location, from south to east.

Fred on top of command outpost (COP) in Alishang District, Lagman Province

In 2005, I was twenty-one years old and had been at war for over a year. I was working with the Tenth Mountain Division from New York. We climbed a hill where there was a big group of Taliban. The U.S. dropped bombs and killed some of them. We ran up the hill to see if any Taliban were still alive. We thought we were safe.

As soon as we neared the top, a Taliban fighter threw something at us that looked like a rock. "Hand grenade! Get cover!" I dove behind one rock, while another soldier took cover behind another rock. A piece of shrapnel hit him in the eye. He was bleeding.

A helicopter landed, picked him up, and took him to Bagram. He was blind in one eye, but he was alive. Times like that made me so sad, because the soldiers were my family. I respected the older ones as I would my father. The younger ones I respected like my brothers. I got so mad if anyone hurt them. It didn't matter to me that the soldiers were from a different country. They were in my country. They were there to help my people.

I was a bridge between the American soldiers and the villagers. If the villagers told me the truth, it helped the soldiers. If they told me lies, it would hurt the soldiers. All I cared about was getting truthful information.

In 2007, I was listening to my scanner and heard Taliban music in a nearby village. The next morning, we went there and found some cassettes. We were trying to find out why they were playing this music. I saw an old, old guy coming back from the bazaar. I asked him, "Do you have a house?"

He said, "I live right here."

"Okay, show us your house."

"Why?"

"Just nothing." He took us to one house and said, "This my house." Then he changed his mind. "Oh, this is not my house. The next one is my house." He was playing with us. He showed us five or six different houses. I knew he was lying. Finally, he took us to a new location and said, "This is my house." The commander sent one of the soldiers to check what was inside. The soldier yelled very loud, "There's a big cache of enemy arms here." We found ten AK-47s, one PKM [a Russian machine gun], one RPG [rocket-propelled grenade], and thousands of rounds of ammunition. They could have killed maybe at least five hundred people with these weapons. A PKM is a big weapon, bigger than an M-4 and an AK-47.

THE PHOTOGRAPH

I'm going to tell you the story about one guy who changed my life. That same year, 2007, I was working for the Arizona National Guard. We were looking for a top leader of the Taliban. His name was M.D. [For Fraidoon's security, only the person's initials are being used here.] M.D. and his men had attacked us many, many times. Many.

It was a rainy spring day. Me, two American soldiers, and an Afghani soldier went to the front gate of the compound to take pictures in front of the scenic mountains.

That night, the pictures were printed. The platoon leader who printed the pictures ran to my room and said, "We have to talk right now."

"Why? What's going on?"

"Do you know this guy, the guy in the background of the picture?"

"No."

"This is M.D. We have to find him and catch him right now."

The enemy was right there with his soldiers, walking, just walking, from one village to the other village. We had taken the picture for fun. We didn't know that he was in the background. I couldn't believe it! "So, let's go find him," I said.

Next morning, when the local workers came to the base, I asked one who had been a good source for me, "Hey, if you find M.D. for me, I will give you anything you want." We had a lot of things at the base: radios, food, oil, clothes.

The photo that changed Fraidoon's life

He said, "Okay."

He went to the bazaar, came back, and said, "He's sitting in the butcher shop right now." I put the picture in my pocket and informed the soldiers. Everybody was ready. We went to the town. As soon as we got close to the town, M.D. tried to run away. Someone must have warned him that the Americans were coming.

He ran inside a nearby cornfield. "Stop!" I shouted. "Come here! I need to talk to you." Because I had a picture of him with me, I knew what he looked like. The clothes he was wearing yesterday were the same ones he had on this day. "Come here," I said.

He came to me. "What's your name?" I asked him.

"My name is M.D."

"Okay, M.D., do you have a couple of minutes to talk to me?" The ten or fifteen Americans who came with me were locked and loaded, ready to shoot if anything happened. Had I been alone, I would have been killed right away.

He was, like, "Yeah, sure."

"Okay, come to the side."

His family already heard that he was going to get captured by United States forces. They climbed up on a roof and watched us. I took him to the side, handcuffed him, and put a cover on his head. "Let's walk," I told him. "Don't do anything stupid. Just walk with me." Both sides of the road were covered by U.S. soldiers. In thirty seconds, the U.S. military convoy took him away.

A few days later, I heard the news. The Taliban had put a fatwa on me. The company commander said to me, "We have heard a report that the Taliban were planning to kidnap you and trade you for M.D. Make sure you do not go anywhere alone."

The timing for this was not good. Here I was with a fatwa at the very time I was trying to get engaged to be married.

4
Who Would Marry Someone with a Fatwa on His Head?

I only told two people in my family that there was a fatwa on me. I told my dad because he was a retired military officer and knew how to handle this kind of situation. I told my brother because he was trying to get a job like mine and is very smart. In Afghanistan, we try to keep sad things from women. What happened to me when I was at work with the American army, what happened to my dad when he was at work with the Afghan National Army, we keep quiet.

Even though I pretended that everything was fine, I walked around feeling that I could die at any minute. I didn't trust anyone outside my family. Everyone looked suspicious to me. Is that man coming on the street going to kill me? Are those guys walking past our house coming for me? To be safe, I moved me and my family from location to location. I made up all kinds of reasons to relocate. "Okay," I would say, trying to look happy and positive, "we've lived here long enough. Let's get a new house." A few months later, I would say, "Let's move to another neighborhood to see what it's like." My brother who knew the real reason for the move always backed me up. "That's a good idea," he would say. We did this over and over again.

Every time I went home on leave, my family said, "Hey, you have a job, you have money, you have a house, you have everything. The only thing you are missing is a wife to make your future better. Make a family for yourself." I thought long and hard about who to marry.

HOMA

Homa is my relative on my mom's side. My mom and Homa's father are cousins. I always liked her. She looked so beautiful. She was fifteen and still in school. Homa knew me a little bit. We had never spent time together.

Homa's father was like a second dad to me. He's a great person, a nice person. Things I could not say to my mom and dad I could say to him. He would then pass along my message to my mom and dad. He was my best friend. One thing I was shy to say to my parents was that I would like to get married.

Homa's father always told me, "In the future, if you want to marry someone, just let me know, I'm going to help you out. I'm going to help to get that girl for you."

I was like, "Okay."

Here's the problem: How could I tell my best friend that I wanted to marry his daughter? How could I say, "Can I marry your daughter?" How could I tell Homa's mom, who is a really good mom, that I wanted Homa? I was not shy in front of the United States Army. I was not shy in front of the enemy. But to marry? That's another story.

One of my uncles on my father's side is the same age as me. I said to him, "Uncle, tell my mom and dad that I would like to marry Homa."

In 2008, my family went to Homa's family and asked, "If it's possible, we would like these two to get married." Her father said, "I don't have any problem. I know Fraidoon for a long time. I like him as my son. I would like to do it. Let's ask Homa."

There were a few other guys who were trying to marry Homa. Her parents asked, "Which one do you want? You have Fraidoon, you have this guy, you have that guy." And Homa said, "I would like to marry Fraidoon." We were all happy.

While this was happening, I was away on a fifteen-day mission. I called home, hoping to get an answer from my uncle. "What happened, Uncle? It has been fifteen days. Did you talk with Homa's family or not?"

"Congratulations," my uncle said. "Your mom is here, your dad is here, all your uncles are here. You are now engaged, and we will celebrate when you get home." I never told Homa or her family about the fatwa. If her family had known, they never would have let me marry their daughter.

Weddings take time in my country. The male's family must save a lot of money to pay for the wedding. They must build a house for the wife.

Throughout their engagement, Fraidoon continued to translate for the Americans. He did not tell Homa about the fatwa.

DAVE

The same year Homa and I became engaged, I was working with different units of the United States Army. One of the people I met was Dave, a retired FBI agent who worked for a security company. Dave was doing some secret stuff and needed a translator. While I was translating for the Pennsylvania National Guard, I also worked for him.

"Dave was doing some secret stuff and needed a translator."

As an FBI agent, Dave had worked on large-scale international drug-trafficking cases in Central America. His strongest skill was an ability to develop informants. Dave was well liked and well connected, a charming character whose self-effacing stories were peppered with irony and a strong sense of justice. After Dave retired from the FBI, he became bored. Having led such an active life, he thought about how he could continue to use his highly developed skills. "I had never served in the military. I felt an obligation to sign up because I knew I had the skills they could use.

"In Afghanistan, I would get calls from informants all hours of the day and night, but I couldn't talk Pashto or Dari. I'd run down to Fred's tent, yelling, 'Terjiman, terjiman,' which means 'interpreter' in Pashto. I'd wake up Fred and hand him the phone. He'd do the interview and take notes while I stood there, doing nothing. When it was over, Fred would write up the notes in English, and from them I'd write my report.

"Fred was so intelligent that I never needed to say, 'Damn, we should have asked him this' or 'We should have asked him that.' Everybody trusted Fred. He was highly sought-after not just because of his honesty but because of his ability to determine if the person he was talking to was telling the truth." The friendship between the two men would eventually lead to a series of momentous events.

The biggest attack was in 2008. Most of the translators had special radios to listen to the enemy's conversation. The radio scanned the area, looking for enemy conversations. At this time, I heard that the Taliban were going to attack our outpost. It was called [Command Outpost] Najil, a very small military base. There were only thirty U.S. soldiers and twenty-five men from the Afghan National Army. The Taliban had more than three hundred people.

I informed the company commander of the Pennsylvania National Guard. "The enemy is going to attack us. Make sure to get ready."

"How do you know?" he asked.

"I know this from their conversation." They were speaking Pashai, a different language that they speak in the valley. It's a completely different language than Pashto, like the difference between English and Spanish. About thirty-five Pashai worked on the base as cleaners. I picked up a word every day.

It was twelve o'clock at night. They shot a few RPGs at the base. Then they shot at us with the PKM, AK-47s. But we were ready for them.

The Pennsylvania National Guard was in position. I was inside a room with my scanner, listening, translating, and passing the information to the commander. I thought, why should I do this in a room? Let me go outside and see what the soldiers are doing. As soon as I went outside, I heard a round coming close to me. I thought I was going to die in a second. Rounds were coming close, really close, practically touching my feet. They were shooting at me, but I wasn't scared. The soldiers were lined up all around the base, shooting back at the enemy. I heard on my radio where their location was. I heard when they were ordered to change directions.

I ran to the commander. "They're going to fire from such-and-such location." Everybody moved to the new location before they started shooting. Then I heard, "Change location. Shoot from south." I informed the commander, "They're going to shoot from south." Everybody charged to the south of the base.

In battle, all you smell is burning. All you see is smoke. You're not able to see maybe five feet from yourself because of the smoke. You cannot smell cigarettes, you cannot smell fresh fruit, you cannot smell trees. You only smell bullets and death. War smells like weapons.

At the end of the battle, thirteen Taliban were killed, and six were injured and captured alive. No casualties for Afghan National Army or the U.S. troops. Everybody was safe. That was the biggest attack I had ever been in.

ONE WEDDING AND TWO FATWAS

Two years after our engagement, Homa and I married. It was a big wedding; 650 people participated in our wedding. My immediate family were ten. Then I have five uncles from my father's side. Each of them has five kids, so everybody's coming. Then they have their families; then we have family members from my mom's side. Then there's Homa's family. Family members came from different parts of the country. So many people come to weddings in Afghanistan. It was a lot of fun.

One morning, maybe twenty days after we were married, Homa was home in Kabul, and I was back in Laghman Province, working as a linguist for the army and for the MEP [Mission Essential Personnel].

While cleaning our yard, Homa found a piece of paper at the bottom of the door. It said, "We know your son is working for the Americans. He's an infidel. We will capture him, and he will die. No one would be dead like him. He would be an example to others who are working for Americans." This was what I wanted to protect my wife from knowing. Homa gave the paper to my dad.

My dad immediately called me. "Do not come home, because someone is trying to kill you. Move to a new location." Homa was safe. They wouldn't hurt my family. I talked to my MEP site manager. "Sir, please transfer me to another part of the country." He agreed.

The next morning, when I went to his office, he said, "We don't have a job for you right now. Go home, and we will call you soon." I was happy that I could go home and spend time with my family. The first thing I did was move us to a new location.

Fraidoon waited and waited. No one called. This wait would have consequences, dangerous consequences, ones he never dreamed could happen.

I waited for the call for two and a half months. I was kind of upset, thinking, "Why aren't they calling me back? I didn't do anything wrong. I just asked for a transfer."

After two years, translators have the choice to select work at a safe place inside the base or on the front line. I worked for six years on the front line of the war and never asked to be inside the base. Why didn't they call me?

Finally Carlo, a very big guy from New York who worked with a private security company, called me. "I have been in Ghazni with the military, in different parts of the country with the military, and heard you're a linguist," he said. "Would you like to work for a private security company?"

"Yeah, sure. What is the main duty?"

"You'll be responsible for the security of American bases." I joined the private security company to become a supervisor. I would be responsible for three hundred armed Afghani security guards on six military bases. For the first half of the month, the Americans trained me. I took classes in such subjects as the rule of law, rules of engagement, and what to do during natural disasters, like floods or snow. I learned what to do if there was at attack at the front gate.

My main job was to make sure security measures for the American forces were properly carried out by my Afghani guards.

Fraidoon's new job was more dangerous than his work as a translator. He drove from one base to another with little protection, in a plain pickup truck or car, providing Afghani security support to American military bases in three provinces and to various embassies in Kabul. He was in charge of two hundred sixty armed guards.

Meanwhile the MEP were reorganizing their books and came upon Fred's name. An unthinkable mistake occurred: someone checked a box on his file

that said "Refusal to go on a mission." This was not true. The MEP had not
called Fred back. This clerical error could have cost him his life.

In 2010, our son, Fardin, was born. I was away, working with security guards at a command outpost called Baraki Barak, in Logar Province. My mom, dad, sister, Homa's mom, dad, and older sister took my wife to the hospital. I was told I had a son the next morning. Now that I was a father, I worried about the well-being of my family. I was always thinking about keeping my family safe. I never thought about me dying or being killed by insurgents. The birth of my son did not stop me from my work. My fight was still against terrorism.

SEPTEMBER 5, 2011

I was driving three Afghan security guards from one outpost or FOB [forward operating base] to another. We were ten minutes away from Baraki Barak when my car was hit by an IED [improvised explosive device]. The car was destroyed. We were all alive but very, very dizzy.

I was a little injured, because we don't care about seat belts in my country. My nose and head were bleeding. There was dust all around me. I was still pushing the gas pedal on what was left of the car. I looked at my military boots. They had been blown off my feet. I was barefoot. I always tied my boots very carefully, but because the explosion was so heavy, they were ripped right off me. My cell phone was gone. People were coming toward us, trying to capture us. I started running, completely out of my mind. I found my cell phone and a gun and threw myself in a ditch.

I shot toward the people while calling the base. "Sir, I blew up with an IED," I told them. The first sergeant from Tenth Mountain Division, New York, immediately announced what happened over the loudspeaker: "Fred was just blown up by an IED!"

"Sir, I blew up with an IED."

I heard them call for a helicopter. I said, "Hey, I'm okay. Just the car blew up. I'm alive, just a little bleeding. My guys are okay. We don't need a helicopter."

"No, we would like to find who did this to you." The troops were on the way.

It was easy to find out who tried to blow us up. I had seen the guy on the road earlier. I remembered a man with a long beard, man jammies, and a white hat, sitting in a tree, just like a chicken. I even said hi to the guy, trying to be respectful. He didn't say hi back; he just sat there, waiting for us to drive by. Then he blew up the IED. I was so upset. I chased the guy while shooting five magazines from my AK-47, a hundred and fifty rounds. But he ran away.

I called my dad. "My vehicle was just blown up by an IED. I'm safe, my friends are safe, the Americans are safe, everyone is safe." Five minutes later, the whole company of soldiers, including four medics, surrounded us. The helicopter arrived and took us to the base.

At the time, I didn't say anything to my mom or Homa. When I went home on vacation, I sat close to them, face-to-face, and told them what had happened. "My car was blown up by an IED, but I'm safe right now. I'm home."

Homa started crying. My mom started crying. My sister started crying. The rest of the family heard about it and came to my house. Homa's sisters were crying. Everyone was crying, especially the females. This is why I did not tell the women about the first fatwa. I knew they would all be crying. I said, "I'm okay. I'm here. Look, nothing happened to me. It's too late to cry. A week ago, maybe cry, but not now."

Homa said, "I made a mistake in my life."

"What's your mistake, Homa?"

"Because I married you."

I said, "Homa, why did you make a mistake to marry me?"

"Because one day you're going to die. You are in the first line of the war and you're going to die. Me and my son will be at home with nobody, with no dad, with no husband. What should we do in the future?

"Take me somewhere with you, anywhere you choose," she said. "Let's go to the mountains — no one will be there, no enemy will be there. We will have a safe place, not a good building, not a good house, just a tent. I will live with you in a tent, but I don't want you to be in a dangerous area like you are now."

Homa continued, "We have everything in Kabul, a house, a car, everything. I don't need these things. I just need security."

"Homa, just wait. Someday, some things will change." She cried so much. The whole night, she was crying. The next day, she was crying. She didn't stop. "Don't cry," I said. "It's over. This is not the first time I was blown up by an IED. In 2004, I was blown up too. I've been in more than a hundred firefights. It's okay."

Homa didn't say anything; she was only crying.

That was it. Even though I wanted to defend my country, I knew I had to make a big change.

5
Coming to America, the Hard Way

Back in 2009, the U.S. military forces encouraged me to take my family to live in a peaceful country, to live in the United States. The soldiers who were already home wrote to me on Facebook: "By 2014, the President of the United States is going to move all the soldiers in Afghanistan back to United States. It's going to get worse for you. Apply today."

I applied to relocate to the U.S. My reason for leaving Afghanistan was security for my family and me. Because of my work for the U.S. military, the Taliban were trying to kill or capture me.

At that time, the policy was to get a background check from the Afghan National Army and Afghan National Police, send the results to the U.S. Embassy, and wait for the call to come for an interview. I did this. There was no call for an interview. For some reason, the envelope was lost in the middle of somewhere.

The next year, I applied for an SIV, Special Immigrant Visa. For some reason, I was denied. I didn't know why.

In April 2014, our daughter, Leema, was born. I was home on vacation, so I was able to take Homa to the hospital. My mom and my older sister came with us. Homa had the baby, and the next morning, we were home. I can't explain the feeling of having a daughter. I love her more than myself.

> Homa asked Fraidoon to translate her feelings at this time. "When the first time I had a son, I was so happy because I was a complete mom, not only a wife, not only a bride, but I was a mom too. I was so excited. When I had Leema, I was even more happy, because I was a mom to two kids — a boy and a girl. My happiness becoming a mom never changed."

By this time, Dave had finished his tour and was back home in Nebraska. He looked for organizations that would help me. After a while, he found the International Refugee Assistance Project (IRAP).

> Dave says that the IRAP was a very small organization, only six full-time paid employees, but they had about four hundred lawyers in their network doing pro bono legal work.

IRAP vetted me, took my case, and provided me with a lawyer, Sari Long. Sari is the best lawyer. She put in a new SIV application for me.

Sari says, "I've cried only once in my professional life, and it was about this case."

> On June 9, 2014, Fraidoon and Sari had their first Skype conference call. Sari says, "I was nervous about talking to him because some of these folks have been terribly traumatized. They've seen things that we can't imagine.

"I've cried only once in my professional life, and it was about this case." (Sari in New York at a later date.)

"Fred didn't open with the fact that he had been blown up by IEDs. He didn't say that he had a letter from the Taliban saying he was going to be killed. He just said how he loved working with the U.S. military. He answered every question I had. He said, 'Whatever you do, I'm so grateful. I've tried doing this on my own and haven't gotten very far. I don't know what the problem is. How can I help?'"

Two paralegals were also working with Sari and Fraidoon during the first Skype call. They started with the basics: "What are you doing now? What have you done?"

Sari says, "Fred smiled a lot on Skype, which was disarming because the previous clients I had worked with were too traumatized to smile. He was so American. He punctuated every other word with fuck *because that's how he had learned to talk from enlisted guys. He was, like, 'I fucking did this, and I fucking did that.' I tried hard not to laugh. I tried to be a professional attorney, but he was such a disarmingly charming person. We talked about his family. He talked a lot about Dave because Dave was his champion, his advocate. During our initial call, we tried to nail down the details about moving forward on the SIV process. First we gathered all of Fred's documentation. Then we needed letters of recommendation from former supervisors to prove that Fred had served faithfully and loyally to the U.S. military and affiliates.*

"Dave put out a call on Facebook. In one day, he got sixty-five responses, which was unbelievable. Usually the hardest part of the application for interpreters is to get letters of support. If I wasn't already convinced that Fred was unique, that confirmed it.

"I touched base with the National Visa Center (NVC) here in the U.S. to determine the status of Fred's case and to inform them that I was his legal representative."

The National Visa Center did not reply. Sari contacted Congressman Mark Pocan of Wisconsin. In seeking a congressional contact, she chose Pocan because Fraidoon served with members of the Wisconsin National Guard, who could say to their representative, "We really, really care about this man. Do what you can." The congressman came on board. So many people were involved in bringing Fred to the States. Sari says, "I wondered about all those poor people who need this program but don't have the support that Fred had earned.

"The National Visa Center's response to me was to ask for more informa-tion. Fred immediately submitted additional information. In July, the NVC said that they had everything they needed. We were feeling good at this point." Two weeks later, Fred's application was denied.

Here is the reason provided for the denial: "Given that your employment was terminated for cause, you do not meet the requirement of faithful and valuable service to the U.S. Government."

Sari explains: "One of the requirements for an SIV is proof that you have had twelve months of 'faithful and valuable service.' If any negative comments are on record, such as you were fired or you had a disciplinary action against you, you will be denied at the very first step of your SIV process. Fred's former employer, Mission Essential Personnel (MEP), did not keep good records. Their records stated that Fred refused to go on a mission.

"'Hey, it says right here that you refused a mission,' I said to Fred. 'Did you refuse a mission? Is there something you're not telling me?'

"Fred got so fired up. I'd never seen him so worked up. 'I HAVE NEVER REFUSED A MISSION,' he shouted. 'I took on more missions than anyone else. I can't believe that's on file. I didn't even notice this.'

"Ultimately, we found out that when Fred requested the transfer because of the threats against his life, they replied, 'We're going to transfer you to

Kabul. Wait for our call. We'll find work for you at the airport. Just hang out for a while.'

"Fred waited a long time, but they never called. It turned out that the records were not up-to-date, and they were calling the wrong telephone number. When Fred didn't answer, they just wrote it up as a refused mission.

"I was on the phone with the lead officer manager in Kabul, who acknowledged that their records were bad. Nevertheless, he refused to do anything about it. He said, 'You're never going to get a new letter.' That's what he told me."

When the office manager told Sari that they didn't have time to deal with Fred, Sari was furious. 'Well," she said, "I have all the time in the world, and I will call you every day until you fix this record." And she did.

"I went to my office at seven in the morning so that I could call MEP in Kabul in the middle of their day. 'Hey, guys, where are you at with this?'

"Dave called too. I think Dave's calls are what ultimately changed their minds. He had been there. He had seen Fred at work."

I didn't tell Homa about this. She was always asking me, "Where's your application?" I'd tell her, "It's under process—just wait." But I was reading e-mails that said, *denied, re-appeal, denied.*

Dave wrote letters for me. He said, "If Fred doesn't have space to live in the U.S., my house is his house. He can live with me." Everybody who tried to help me was pissed.

Sari continues: "Finally, one person at MEP had the wherewithal to look at the pay records and the transfer records for the contracting company. They saw the error and agreed to change their letter."

In August 2014, Sari submitted an appeal for Fred's case, along with a new MEP letter with the corrected reason for termination: no position available.

Command Sergeant Major Paul Metz got Wisconsin senator Tammy Baldwin involved. She provided a letter of support for Fred's appeal. At this point, they were appealing the denial based on the fact that the Mission Essential Personnel had screwed up.

Sari wasn't convinced that an appeal would work. "I submitted a second, entirely new application, with all the correct answers. My thinking was, they could deny the appeal, but they could not deny a fresh, totally correct application.

"We waited and waited and still got nothing. We had submitted this stuff in August and September. No response."

During the years of waiting, Fraidoon continued his dangerous work with the security company. The fatwa was still in place.

Sari says, "The National Visa Center and the U.S. Embassy in Kabul were completely nonresponsive in any of the follow-ups that we were trying to get. Senator Baldwin's office stayed involved. Finally, in April, the National Visa Center said, 'We have everything we need.' At last we were on the way.

"Two weeks later, the National Visa Center denied both the appeal and the second application. They said—and this is the worst part about the whole process—they said, 'Derogatory information has been associated with Fraidoon Akhtari that is incompatible with the regulations of the SIV program.' That's when I cried at work."

6
The Black Hole
of Red Tape

When "derogatory information" is cited as the reason for visa refusal, the application goes into a black hole. Sari says, "You will never find out what is on the record. It could have been a disgruntled colleague that called the embassy, and says, 'Fraidoon, he worked for the Taliban.' It could have been anything or anyone. They'll never tell you what it is."

At that point, Fred was ready to give up. "I'm done. What can I do now? There's nothing I can do." But Sari and Dave would not give up. They tapped everybody they knew. Sari spoke with generals and other military people to find the latest information. She went to immigration conferences and asked officials from the U.S. Citizen and Immigration Services and from the National Visa Center how to get out of the black hole. Dave used his considerable contacts to call a general and the FBI legal attaché in Kabul.

Dave says, "One general — I'm not going to say his name because I don't think that he would want this to be known — agreed to meet Fred in Kabul and do a detailed security background check. If there was anything that pinged on that background check, we would know what the issue was. We would know what was in the black hole. The general ran a background check, and not a single problem showed up."

During this process, a second U.S. senator, Bill Cassidy, from Louisiana, became involved. Sari says, "Senator Cassidy had no connection with this fight, no constituents who worked with Fred in Afghanistan. But his office did more than any other in terms of getting information. I believe he agreed to help because Dave's brother is a bigwig attorney in Louisiana.

"We wrote several letters to Secretary of State John Kerry, and later to Secretary of State Rex Tillerson." No stone was left unturned.

By August 2015, a year after the appeal and second application had been filed, Sari filed a new appeal, citing the general's background check. Dave adds, "There was no formal citation because we couldn't say who ran the background check. We could only say that it happened.

"In February 2016, we got the chief of mission's approval for the case. We then submitted the petition to the Immigration Service."

In June, the petition was approved. Sari and Dave were notified that Fred had a visa appointment on November 28, 2016. Everything went well at the visa appointment. Finally, finally, finally, Fred would be approved.

Not. Quite. Yet.

Congress authorizes only a limited number of visas for the SIV program. These visas were quickly running out. Sari said that her heart stopped anytime news came out that the government was running out of visas. Even as they were getting closer to the time when Fred could be issued a visa, she knew that there might not be any visas left.

Sari says, "My law firm has lobbyists who began lobbying on a pro bono basis for more visas, because this wasn't a problem that only Fred was experiencing. Everybody applying for the SIV program faced incredible delays. At the last minute, Congress came through and authorized more visas.

"Through it all, Fred was never self-pitying. He was never not trusting of the work that we were doing. Everybody wanted to help. His story was just too sympathetic. You can't read the letters from the American soldiers he worked with and not feel compelled to help."

My case was approved after five different applications. It took seven years. I kept working with the Americans until July 13, 2017, two days before flying here.

When Fraidoon's visa finally came through, he sent Sari a picture of it. She says, "I didn't wait for the State Department and the IOM [International Organization for Migration] to buy the airline tickets. No way! No more waiting." Sari and Dave called in the troops.

Dave Shiner, a soldier from the Pennsylvania National Guard, immediately started a GoFundMe campaign. "I couldn't believe it," Fred says. "The visa was barely dry on my passport before thousands of dollars were raised. The next week we bought four tickets to America. But the soldiers kept raising money. They bought me a car with the extra cash."

After I went to the U.S. Embassy to pick up my visa, I went straight to see my boss at the security company. "Sir, I'm going to quit." I didn't say the reason. He said, "Look Fred, if you want more money, we would like to pay you. Stay with us." He thought I was going to get another job with another company.

"Sir, it's not about money." I showed him the visa. "This is my visa. This is my ticket to America. This is where I'm going to live. I don't like to leave you alone here, but I did this for the last fourteen years. Now I would like to go."

The commander gave me two months' extra salary. Yeah. I worked until the thirteenth of July, the day before my new life began.

That night, I wrote to my friends on Facebook: "Finally issued!" Everybody was happy. Some of the soldiers I worked with wrote some good jokes. Some wrote good comments, happy comments.

The next day, we were ready to fly. Homa, the children, and I went to the Kabul International Airport with our families — my mom, my dad, my brothers, my sister, Homa's mom, dad, brothers, sisters, my uncles, and my brother-in-law. It was hard to say goodbye.

JULY 15, 2017

From Kabul airport, we flew to New Delhi, India. After an eight-hour layover, we flew directly to Dulles International Airport, in Washington, D.C. Before we landed, I told Homa, "Homa, a few friends of mine might be at the airport. They want to welcome me to the U.S." I was expecting maybe five or six people. When we arrived, I went to pick up our bags, and someone had damaged my big suitcase. I was so upset about it. A police officer sent me to a complaint department.

As soon as I finished filling out all the documents in the airport, I went outside. Someone called out, "Welcome home, Fred!" I look around. Who is he? Josh W., from 2008. He had a black beard now and looked completely different. Then I saw twenty people from the Pennsylvania National Guard unit. People from 2005, from the 82nd Airborne Division, North Carolina, were there. They left their homes at three o'clock in the morning just to say hi.

Sari was there. We finally got to meet. Dave was at the airport too. He flew in from Nebraska just to bring us home. So many of the great people I met in Afghanistan were there.

Sari says, "That morning at Dulles airport was the first time I met Dave in person. We probably spoke on the phone at least once a week throughout the years we worked on this. He's such a character. Meeting Dave was amazing, especially knowing that in an hour, Fred would be showing up too.

"When Fred walked out of the arrival area, oh, my, I've never felt so much relief. I was convinced that Fred would face a ton of scrutiny when he presented his SIV in Washington, D.C. Thankfully he did not.

"Homa and the kids were happy, relaxed, and grateful. I'm sure that they hadn't thought very much about how their lives were going to change. How could you possibly anticipate that? They'd left everything they knew, and now they were here. They didn't know what their apartment would look like. They didn't know what jobs they'd have. But they didn't care, because after so many years, they were here.

"People wonder, if Fred had threats for so many years, how come the Taliban didn't kill him? They tried. But it wasn't like the Taliban had all the time in the world to go door-to-door looking for him every day.

"At no point did Fred think that the U.S. military wasn't doing the right thing. At no point did he criticize the military or the U.S. government for delaying and messing up the interpreters' SIV process. At no point did he ever say anything like that, which was not how I felt. I was angry the entire time. Multiple times I had KAYAK up on my computer screen, looking for round-trip tickets to Kabul, because I wanted to go myself and talk to the ambassador. I wanted to talk to Mission Essential Personnel. And if need be, I wanted to kick them in the shins, because what they were doing was astonishingly unjust."

"I'm feeling so good, yeah. I'm so happy."

From Dulles, we flew to Chicago. We stayed there for a couple of hours and then took a flight to Nebraska. We had been traveling for thirty hours. I thought Nebraska was going to be a calm place. I thought that I would get off the airplane, sit in a car, go to my new home, and rest. But when I got there, everybody was there. Some people we knew and others we did not know. They made us feel welcome in Nebraska.

Our home is very happy. Since we've been here, we've seen no armored vehicles, no guns, no explosions, no helicopters, no military convoys. Everyone is safe. The only thing we saw were a couple of kids playing with fake guns. Homa is going to school to learn English. The school has a place for the children while Homa studies. She's making friends with students from all over the world. Fardin goes to school. He's learning English fast. I am working for a private security company, but this time the job is different. My main responsibility is to watch over the security for Facebook's database in Omaha.

I didn't think about this life for myself, not ever and ever. I wanted it for my kids and for my wife. They needed to live somewhere peaceful. For me, I don't care. I can live in the middle of nowhere. But my wife and kids must live in peace. That was our first day of living in peace.

I told Homa, "We have to take care of the kids. We have to let the kids grow up not like me, not like you. They should grow up like kids here. They should be educated. They should go to a good college. They should learn a lot of things."

I'm feeling so good, yeah. I'm so happy. My life here is completely different. In one and a half months, I have a job, Social Security, a driver's license, and a green card. Homa is even happier than me. She says that Nebraska is the best place. I asked her, "Do you still think you made a mistake to marry me?"

"No, now you're good."

"Nebraska is the best place."

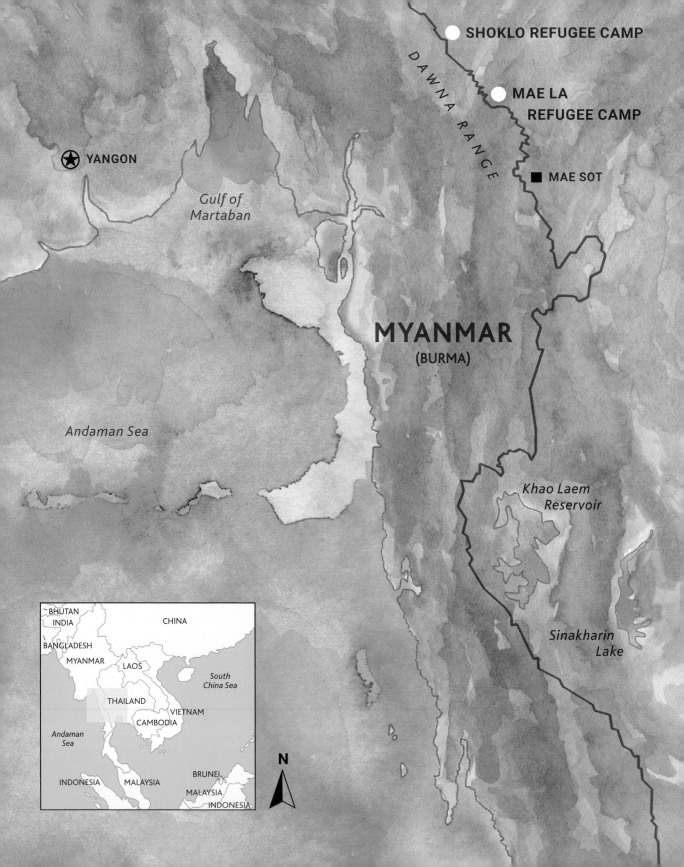

PART II
BIRTH

Nathan

COUNTRY OF ORIGIN:
Myanmar/Thailand

ETHNIC GROUP:
Karen

THAILAND

 **BANGKOK**

Gulf of Thailand

Nathan

7
Flip-Flops, Rice, Soccer

Most refugees have no option but to flee their country if their government cannot protect them from war and persecution. When guns, bombs, machetes, fire, and evildoers are coming every which way, they must RUN. There is little to no time to collect clothing, food, personal mementos, or money. RUN. Run where?

When events such as these happen, often a neighboring country steps up to help. The host country, with aid from the United Nations High Commissioner for Refugees (UNHCR), the Red Cross, or other nongovernmental organizations (NGOs), sets up temporary camps to house and feed the displaced people.

The Karens (pronounced KAH-renz), the second-largest ethnic group in Myanmar (formerly known as Burma), are a case in point. The Karens have been brutally persecuted by the Bamar (also known as the Burmans), who have controlled the government for decades. Although the Karens fight back, they are no match for the country's large, well-armed army. Thousands of Karen refugees have had to cross the border into Thailand and live in temporary refugee camps. Nathan is one of those people.

Nathan says, "Refugees do not want to live in camps. They want to be free to travel, make a living, build a real house, have their own rice field. A refugee camp is not a place where lazy people live, waiting for a handout. We're there because we have no other options. We're there because we are fleeing wars. We're there because we were oppressed in our native country for religious reasons, for ethnic reasons, for all kinds of reasons. As a child, though, I did not understand this. I was just a kid doing things other kids did."

I was born in the Shoklo Refugee Camp, on the Thai side of the border between Thailand and Myanmar. My parents were married for ten years before they had me. They named me Hei Blut. Hei Blut means "gift from God." When I became an American citizen, I looked for a new name that had a similar meaning. Nathan in Hebrew means "He gave." I thought, that's a fine name. "He gave" is like "a gift from God." So I became Nathan.

My dad's name is Billy. He could not speak a word of English, but he has an English name. He was named after a Christian missionary. My mom's name is Eh Ku, which represents "love" in Karen. My brothers and sisters all kept their Karen names.

I grew up like a regular kid, doing normal kid stuff. I didn't know that there was any other way of life. We had our own house, more like a hut, that was made of bamboo with teak leaves for the roof. I had lots of friends, and my grandparents, my mom's parents, lived with us. I was a happy child. My dad worked across the border in Myanmar, building barracks for the Karen army, the KNLA, and was often away.

In 1995, not long after I was born, our camp was burned down by a group of rebels. Everything happened in a split second. There was no time to pack anything, including money, or to prepare for evacuation. My mom, my grandparents, and I just ran. This was hard, especially for my grandmother. She had hidden all her money above her sleeping place. Everyone told her that it was not a safe place for money, but she refused to listen. She wanted to be able to reach up and touch her money. She lost all of it in a fiery bed.

We hid in a big cave crowded with people from the camp. The rebels returned again and again, burning more sections of Shoklo. My mother later told me that I was a very good baby-in-hiding. Although I was not even a year old, I didn't make a peep.

Thai security forces could not protect all the camps, so they moved about fifty thousand of us deeper into Thailand, into one large camp called Mae La. It was sponsored by the U.N. Other ethnic groups escaping repression moved there too, but mostly they were Karen refugees. We had to build a new house from scratch, again using bamboo for the sides and floor, and leaves from the palm trees for a roof.

BASICS

The new camp, the place where I lived much of my life, was surrounded by barbed wire. We were not allowed to go outside the barbed-wire compound without a Thai ID. Thai IDs were very expensive, and we were very poor, so we could not leave. The U.N. provided the basics — rice, vegetable oil, beans, charcoal, and water — based on how many people were in the family. The rest was up to us. But the thing is, the free stuff they gave us was not enough to feed five members in a family. If you didn't work, you didn't have enough food, you didn't have shoes, you didn't have clothes, you didn't have money to pay for an education. (We had to pay to go to day care and

Nathan's family in front of their house in Omaha, Nebraska (back row, left to right): Hel But Say (his brother, 17), Eh Ku (his mom), Billy (his dad), Nathan, 23; (front row, left to right): Helblu L Htoo and Helblu L Say (his twin siblings, 13), Hei Blut Laura Paw (his sister, 10)

to school.) There was a limited amount of work in the camp. Very limited. So where else can you earn money to feed your family?

My mom was a librarian. She made five hundred baht, about twenty dollars, a month. She was grateful for her job, but it wasn't enough to feed a family, so she also raised chickens and rabbits. My dad was a self-taught carpenter. To make money, he would sneak out of the camp and walk back to Myanmar. If he got caught outside the camp, he would go to jail or be shot. There were other dangers in Myanmar, like land mines and getting caught in the cross fire during an attack. But my dad went anyway and was gone for months at a time.

Somehow my mom always knew when my dad was coming home. I don't know how she knew this, because we didn't have a phone or anything. Me and my friends would wait for him at the barbed-wire gate. My dad was very generous. He always handed us some money, one baht, five baht. Then me and my dad would walk home together. Even though my parents had so little, they always found ways to provide for me and my siblings.

When I turned seven, my mom started teaching me how to do chores: get water from the public pump, make the fire for cooking, cook, and watch my little brother, and later, my other siblings. When Dad was home, though, he did those chores so that I had time to play. He worried about my growth because I was so skinny and little.

The camp was divided into zones: Zone A, Zone B, et cetera. Each neighborhood had its own grocery store, but the items there were expensive. Zone C had a big morning market where food and clothes were sold. Thai farmers sold fruits and vegetables. We lived in Zone B. We woke up early in the morning to walk to Zone C in time to get the vegetables. Usually there was a long line at the water pumps, so some people created their own private wells. We didn't have our own well, but one of our neighbors did. They let us come by to shower.

Ours wasn't the nicest house on the block, but it was big, and on stilts high off the ground. All the houses were on stilts because of the monsoons. Me and my friends played underneath the houses. My dad built an area outside for the purpose of cooking. We cooked on the ground, using firewood or charcoal. We had dishes and spoons but mostly we ate with our hands. He also built a bathroom outside the house — an outhouse.

The lights for the camp were turned off at nine p.m. We didn't have electricity, but we had batteries and candles. At night, we slept under mosquito nets. In Thailand, especially during the monsoon season, bugs are part of everyday life.

Even though the camp was large, about 2.4 square kilometers, there was no ordinary transportation inside it. I mean, there were people who had bikes, but we couldn't afford one. The only time we were allowed outside of the barbed-wire fence was to take a taxi that drove around the perimeter of the camp. We couldn't afford to be driven from our area of the camp to the other side. We walked.

There were three hospitals for fifty thousand people. The hospitals were free but nowhere near the quality of the hospitals in a country like America. There were no operating rooms. If you needed an operation, you had to go to the nearest city. That was quite a drive. And also, the hospital was overcrowded. When I was little, I got sick. My dad carried me on his back to and from the hospital, almost an hour's walk.

MUD

Our school had no windows. There weren't even walls. We used natural light. The floor was mud. There was a long wooden board, like a table, with no chairs, just benches. That's where we did our lessons. NGOs from other nations gave us books, paper, and pens. We all wore white uniforms. The camp didn't have paved roads, just dirt roads, and during the monsoon season, it would get very muddy and slippery. School was about a twenty-minute walk from our house. We couldn't afford rain boots or real shoes; we wore slippers or flip-flops. Once, when I was in the fourth grade, I slipped and fell and got very dirty. It was too late to go back and change my shirt. If I was late for school, I knew that I'd get a spanking. I went to a public water well and washed out the mud, then sat in school, soaked.

Students there showed much more respect to their teachers than they do here. When a teacher entered a room, we stood up and said, "Good morning, teacher." Otherwise, school was just like it is here, with teachers, a principal, and an assistant principal. We learned English right from the start. We learned vocabulary. We did not learn to speak Thai until fifth grade. We studied Burmese, Karen, English, geography, science, and math. But the teachers were nowhere near as learned as here in America.

My parents were really keen on education. They wouldn't let me out of the house unless I studied first. I'd come home from school, shower, eat something, and then study for one or two hours. After studying, they'd let me out to play marbles, tag, soccer — I loved soccer — with my friends. Students were ranked according to their test scores. If I wasn't ranked in the top three, my parents would be really disappointed. I didn't like to disappoint my parents.

One thing that was different there is that the teachers and the principal were allowed to hit you. Parents encouraged this. My parents told the teacher, "If he's bad, if he's misbehaving, make sure you hit him." The teacher gave out twenty English vocabulary words. We had to memorize the words, the spelling and meaning. The next day, we were tested. If you missed one, you were hit one time. If you missed two words, you were hit twice. Once I missed two.

The one thing I was not allowed to do was go outside the barbed-wire fence. My parents explained to me over and over again that once a person was outside the camp, there was no security. It wasn't a war zone, so we didn't have to worry about land mines nearby, but we did have to worry about getting kidnapped. We could be snatched and sold into child slavery. It happened. That was my parents' biggest worry, someone snatching me if I was outside the camp. Also, there were people from Bangkok who came to the camp and told parents about work opportunities for their children. They'd say, "Don't worry about an ID. We'll provide that for them." Once the child was out of the camp, he was gone. He was never again seen. And there was nothing the parents could do, because they didn't have identity cards to leave the camp and search for their child.

The thing is, I liked leaving the camp and going into the jungle. I liked to hunt for things with my slingshot, even though I was terrible at it. One day, my friends and I snuck out to hunt. It wasn't that difficult for us kids to sneak out. I didn't tell my mom, because I knew that I'd be in so much trouble. But I thought that if I brought back wood for the fire — because in the winter it was cold, and our family would sit around a bonfire in the morning — she would forgive me.

When I got home, my mom immediately knew where I had been. "Why did you go so far? Do you know how dangerous that is?" I presented the wood to her as a peace offering. She used a log to spank me.

During the monsoons, the kids loved to play in the mud. That was the most fun we had. We'd go up a muddy hilltop and slide down. When we went home all dirty and sticky with mud, our parents would get mad because they had to wash our clothes. We'd get yelled at and spanked, but it was worth it. Sometimes we slid down the hill so hard our pants ripped. That's when our parents got really mad because they had to buy new clothes. We'd get spanked harder, but it was still worth it.

My happiest memory has got to be Christmastime. Christmas was a community thing rather than just a family thing. It wasn't about one family giving each other presents; it was about many families celebrating together. There was caroling. Afterwards, the carolers came into our house for food that my mom had prepared. We didn't have lights, Christmas lights, we used candles, beautiful candles, all around the house. There were no Christmas trees, but we watched free movies throughout the Christmas season. On Christmas Eve, there was a concert, and Santa Claus came out on the stage and gave us kids candies. At midnight, we ate chicken porridge. On Christmas Day, everybody went to church to worship.

Refugee camps were never intended to be a permanent solution for displaced persons, even when the people in the camp tried their best to create a sense of normalcy and community. It was clear from the start that living in Thailand was a minimal and temporary condition. The refugees there had little to no future. Returning to Myanmar was not an option; the Bamar were still in bloody conflict with the country's ethnic minorities. The only viable alternative was to resettle in a third country. That process takes years. No one can be resettled without thorough vetting — an examination into the health and background of the refugee and family. Those who pass are eventually offered a permanent home in a third country.

After years of interviews, waiting, more interviews, more waiting, Nathan finally learned that he and his family would be resettled in the United States. For the first time in his life, Nathan would live in a country he could call his own. For the first time in his life, Nathan and his sisters and brothers had a future.

The year 2005 was a boom time for immigration. People were leaving the camp right and left, and going to Canada, Australia, the U.K., and America. The only sad part about it was that my friends left before me. Would I see them again? Would I be left behind? My parents applied to go to America and Australia. We waited. We waited.

In 2007, I was twelve years old and in the fifth grade. I had changed to a different school, Mission High School, that was known for providing a better education than the school I had been attending. It was expensive, and my parents gave up much of their savings to enroll me there. After about five months, my parents got a letter saying that we were accepted by the United States. My parents were very happy. They thought that life in America would be good for their kids. I was ecstatic. I knew about America because we read about it in books, newspapers, and magazines. We saw what it looked like in movies.

We had a few DVDs, but we didn't own a DVD player. We'd go to a neighbor's house to watch them. There was this movie where a snowman came to life. Frosty. *Frosty the Snowman.* Because of *Frosty the Snowman,* I always wanted to see snow, so I was very excited to come here.

Once I found out that we were leaving, I started skipping school. My parents didn't know about this. Here they were, paying a lot of money to send me to this school, and I was skipping. I thought, I'm going to America; I don't need to go to classes anymore. I played in a cave or at the soccer complex. I was going to America!

8
TV, Hamburgers, Football

Before traveling to the United States, everyone in the family had to pass addi-
tional medical exams and attend orientation classes. The kids were put into
three groups — called Spider-Man, Batman, and Superman — where they
were taught about airplanes, superheroes, and the different appliances found
in American homes. They learned about American foods, like burgers, hot
dogs, and pizza. Nathan learned that in America it was illegal for a teacher to
hit a student. "Really? Is this true? I was in heaven."

The community center had papered the walls with pictures sent by people
who had already emigrated. Nathan was amazed that people had TVs and ice
in their own houses.

The kids in my orientation group were so excited about going to America. Sadly we were all assigned to different states and would no longer see each other every day. My family was assigned to the state of Texas, in a city called Houston.

For the journey, we went by bus to Mae Sot, an hour away from Bangkok. Escorts had been set up in advance to meet us at every stop along the way until we arrived in America. My dad had bought shoes for us back in the camp. Shoes were very expensive, so my parents only bought them for us kids; they wore their flip-flops. But once we reached Mae Sot, we were each given a new pair of shoes. My brother Hel was the only one whose shoes were the correct size. Mine were too big for me, but I wore them anyway. They gave us pants and T-shirts. They gave Mom and Dad jackets too. Other than that, we just wore our regular clothes.

We moved on to Bangkok, where we spent two days, one night, in a hotel. I was in awe of the tall buildings. I had seen tall buildings in the movies but never in person. There was a TV in the hotel bedroom. I never had a TV, much less in the bedroom, and I stayed up all night watching it. We also never had a bathroom in our house. We had an outhouse. "What? Why do we have a bathroom right near where we're sleeping?" We thought that the idea of someone pooping near where you slept was weird.

At the Bangkok International Airport, my mom would not use the escalator. It was too scary. We had to use the stairs. We carried all our luggage. The twins were three years old, so my parents carried them and my other sister, Hei Blut Laura Paw, who was only six months old. Hel and I helped with the luggage.

Every time a helicopter had come to the camp, we kids would run outside and wave to the pilot, so I knew all about helicopters. But airplanes? I had never seen an airplane. Airplanes amazed me. How could something so big be lighter than air? Wouldn't it fall down, carrying so many people? Once I got in and sat in my seat, it didn't feel like I was on a plane flying through the sky. I was, like, in a chair someplace. The flight was long, and the food was strange. I think they gave us hot dogs; they smelled terrible. There were video games, but I didn't know how to mess with the remote. I slept a lot.

We arrived in L.A., our first American stop. At an airport restaurant, we bought fried rice with chicken. I was really, really happy to finally eat rice. The special part for me was seeing all the people in the airports. Living in a refugee camp, I had never seen so many different-looking people in one place—different clothing, different skin color, different hair color. My mother thought that everybody was huge. In the camp, there might be two people who were six feet tall. It seemed that here everyone was a giant.

At this point, we were on our own. No more guides. We went to a video screen and just stood there staring at it. We had no idea what anything meant. A person who worked at the airport stopped and asked us where we were going. I said *House-ton.* "Oh, you mean *Hyoooston*?" And he escorted us to our terminal.

HYOOOSTON

In Houston, our sponsor met us at the airport. He was a white male, and his wife was Burmese. They drove us to our new apartment and showed us how everything worked—the lights, the microwave, the fridge. "Okay, there's food in the fridge. There's food in the pantry. Here's some dishes. Here's how you turn on the stove." And then they were, like, "All right, see you later," or *never*.

I didn't like this new place. This place was very small. Although we didn't have as nice a house in Thailand, we had plenty of room. Here there were only two bedrooms, small for a family of seven. Everything was too different. I wanted to go home. But there was no way to go back. I cried. The twins wanted to go home too. They thought we were just on a trip. "Can we go home now?" they asked.

It was midnight when we reached Houston, but it was only twelve o'clock in the afternoon in Thailand, so we were wide awake. We didn't sleep until morning.

The beds still had on their plastic covering. We didn't know that you were supposed to take off the plastic. When we tried to sleep, the plastic made a lot of noise. My mom got a blanket and laid it on the floor. My dad tried to sleep on the bed, but it made too much noise, so he moved to the floor with us. The beds took a period of adjustment. We slept on the floor for the first couple of days.

Eventually we tried sleeping on the beds, but I fell off a few times. There was a carpet underneath, so it wasn't a hard landing. The restroom was nice. I got used to the restroom pretty fast. I loved the shower.

We had been told that in America, there were mostly white people. But at our apartment complex, there were only a few white people, mostly Hispanics and African Americans. I was like, "Wait, where're all the white people?" I never knew there was such a group as Mexicans, because they didn't teach us about them in the orientation meeting. They spoke a weird-sounding language that I didn't understand at all. I asked my dad about it. "Oh, they're speaking Mexican because they are from a country called Mexico." I don't know how he knew this.

My mom and dad both cook, and there were lots of places to buy Asian food in Houston, so food was no big deal. What was a big deal was getting the food. Going grocery shopping was a twenty- to thirty-minute walk to Walmart. We were used to walking and Houston was flat, so that part wasn't tough. What was tough was crossing the wide streets with all the little ones and a cart filled with groceries. Houston was such a big city, and there were so many cars. Yes, crossing streets was tough.

After the first night, when the sponsor dropped us off at the apartment, we never heard from him again. We were told that some agency would send a caseworker to help us get established. The caseworker never showed up. We didn't have anybody to complain to. We didn't know anything. I wanted to go to school because

I didn't have any friends. I'm a very social person, the extrovert in the family. I was used to having lots of friends, so I was lonely. I thought, maybe when I go to school, I might meet people my age. It was three months before I went to school.

Luckily there were four other Karen families already living in our apartment complex. They helped us the most. They told their caseworkers about us, and their agency sent us a Karen lady who signed me up for school. I liked going to school, but it was strange how the kids talked back to their teachers. At the refugee camp, the teachers had complete power over their students. You did not disrespect your teachers at all. Here, the teachers had little power over their students.

My dad immediately started looking for a job. It was hard to find work in Houston, because he didn't speak English. There was a Karen community in Port Lavaca, two hours away, that hired workers for a big plastics factory. You didn't need to know English to work there. My dad worked in the factory's production line, working a twelve-hour shift, making nine dollars an hour. Not bad. He moved to Port Lavaca so that he could work, and we stayed in Houston. My mom stayed home, taking care of the younger kids.

I was put into the fifth grade. My English wasn't very good, and sometimes the kids made fun of the way I talked, but it wasn't anything that crushed my spirit. School was the place where I could interact with people my age, so it was worth a little teasing. After school was the sad time for me. There wasn't a playground where I could play with my friends like there was in Thailand. I couldn't go to a friend's house and say, "Hey, come out and play." And there wasn't as much home-work to do as there was in the camp. I got that done real quick.

I'd go to the park and walk around by myself or just stay home. After my dad was working for a while, he bought us a TV. I was excited. I didn't want to go out after that. In Thailand, you have to pay to see a movie. Now I could stay home and watch movies all day. We didn't know the English well enough to understand what was happening, but it didn't matter. We mostly watched a Hispanic channel that showed American movies with a Spanish voice-over. We couldn't afford cable, and that was the only channel that showed movies all day.

My parents met other refugee families from Thailand camps. I became friends with their kids. I also made friends with a Pakistani kid who had also grown up in a refugee camp. Back in Thailand, we had heard rumors that people in the South and the Midwest didn't like immigrants, but we met lots of nice, generous people wherever we stayed.

We only lived in Houston for five months. A large beef-packing company was short on employees. They heard about the refugees in Houston and offered jobs to a couple hundred families. But the company was eleven and a half hours away, in a town called Cactus. They sent buses to pick us up. U-Haul trucks took everyone's stuff.

CACTUS/AMARILLO

Cactus was a way too small town for us. There was not even a downtown, just two gas stations. The only available school in the town was an elementary school, no middle or high schools. But the meatpacking company was there. My dad was able to make enough to take care of us, send money back to relatives still in the camp, and buy a car, a Ford minivan. At first, he was the only one in the family who knew how to drive. He had to drive us to another town just to go to Walmart.

I started speaking English really well, and I started making friends. I fell in love with football. Not soccer, American football. I begged my mother to let me go out for the team. She would not allow me to play. She thought it was too violent. She said, "You can play soccer. You can play baseball. You can wrestle. No, no, no. No football."

My dad decided that there would be more opportunities for us in a bigger place. Amarillo had two hundred thousand people — not too big, not too small.

The next year, we moved to Amarillo. My dad still didn't speak English and he didn't have a degree. Remember, he was a self-taught carpenter. But he could get a job at Tyson's meatpacking company. Since the twins were in school, my mother got a job cutting meat at Tyson's too. She hired someone to take care of Hei Blut Laura Paw, who was still too young for school.

We lived in Amarillo for more than four years. During that time, I did well in school, making honor roll every year. I connected with my teachers who were Americans and made friends with all kinds of people — whites, blacks, Hispanics, and Asians.

In 2011, when I was a freshman in high school, some of my soccer friends and I drove to Omaha, Nebraska, for the weekend to attend Karen Martyrs' Day. Every year we celebrate our leaders that gave their lives for our people. We have a memorial, a soccer tournament, and concerts. Omaha has a large Karen population, and the celebration was held there from 2009 to 2012.

I stayed with an aunt and cousin. My cousin worked for Omaha Public Schools, in the Migrant Education Program. She told me that there were lots of opportunities in Omaha, and if I were to live here, there were lots of migrant programs to help kids go to college. Then I met other Karen kids in Omaha who had scholarships for the university.

Back home, I told my parents that I would like to move to Omaha. I told them that I wanted to go to a university, and that there were more scholarship opportunities in Omaha. My parents quickly agreed to move. It was not difficult for them to make this decision. They had crossed the world just so me and my siblings would have more opportunities. This was one more risk they were willing to take.

OMAHA

For the first month, we stayed with one of my dad's cousins, and then we found an apartment. There was a Tyson's meatpacking plant in Omaha too, so my dad was able to transfer. My mom, who had worked in Amarillo, was looking forward to staying home to take care of the younger kids. After a while — I'm not sure how long — my dad changed jobs and cut meat in a plant in Fremont, Nebraska, about an hour's drive.

One morning, during our second year in Omaha, my dad woke up and said that he felt numb. Then he couldn't walk, and he couldn't speak. My mom woke me up. "We need to call an ambulance." I didn't want to wait for an ambulance, so we got him into the car and I drove to the emergency room. I was worried during the drive because I didn't know what his condition was. The doctor told us that he had had a stroke. Luckily we caught the stroke early.

The hospital stay was very expensive — almost thirty thousand dollars for three days. My dad's job had provided health insurance, but it barely covered anything. A white lady from Valentine, Nebraska, helped my dad get Medicaid to take care of his continuing medical bills. Her name is Sarah. She was a social worker from Lutheran Family Services.

I was elated when my dad was released from the hospital. He began doing rehab. The Lutheran Family Services and another group, the Migrant Education Program, provided him with an English tutor. The tutor was a Vietnam veteran and really clicked with my dad. They talked a lot about wars. My dad was grateful to him and they've stayed friends. But we still needed to pay the rent and buy food. My mom's very courageous. Even though she depended on my dad, she always knew that she could step up and provide for our family. She got a job working on the production line at a meatpacking company called Hormel Foods.

My dad was angry at the whole situation. He always took pride providing for his family. And besides, he never liked Omaha as much as I did. He thought it was too confined, not like Texas, which was wide open and big. He felt cramped in Omaha. I don't know how to explain it. He didn't have a lot of friends, because he's introverted. His brother lives here, and they see each other, but they don't talk much. They are quiet people.

My parents had been happy in Texas, where they had friends and good jobs. They moved to Omaha, where it is very cold, and very flat, and where they had to start all over again, for me. They moved here just so that I could pursue a scholarship and go to a four-year university. My parents had moved to America because they wanted their kids to have a better future. They came here knowing they would have to work at harsh jobs, like meatpacking, where you stand eight hours a day, get a fifteen-minute break, and do the same thing over and over and over. There was pressure on me to study hard. If I didn't win this scholarship, my parents would have moved for absolutely no reason.

During that same year, my junior year in high school, I heard that the Susan T. Buffett Scholarship paid full college tuition for students who lived in Nebraska. If I could get this scholarship, I wouldn't have to take out loans for school. Not only did you need to have good grades — I had good grades — but you had to show that you were involved in the community.

I joined Thrive, an immigrant leadership club that comes up with projects to help the community. Thinking back to how hard it was when we first arrived in America, I knew firsthand what refugees go through adjusting to a new country, a new culture. For my project, I joined a group of students who helped newly arriving immigrants. The plan was to let the refugees know that there were people in this community who cared about them. We partnered with Lutheran Family Services and the Omaha Fire Department and got a grant from the Migrant Education Program to buy groceries, clothes, and toys for newly arriving families.

Our first family were Karens. A firefighter helped us with donations of furniture and beds. We picked up the family at the airport, took them to their new house, and showed them how things worked. Then we did follow-ups — went grocery shopping, set the kids up in school, and went to the doctor's. I stopped by their apartment once a week to teach them English. It gave me satisfaction, knowing that I made someone's transition a little bit easier. It would have been wonderful to have had people come to our house when we first moved here; just play games with us or take us to a museum or the movies. We had no one. We had to go grocery shopping by ourselves. We had to make friends on our own.

While I was in high school, I became even more involved with the Karen community. I got a job as a translator for the Omaha Public Schools and the local hospitals. They paid me to translate at parent-teacher conferences. My second job was a cook at the Salween Thai restaurant in Omaha. My third job is as a receptionist and mentor to freshmen who have Buffett Scholarships. These jobs continue.

At the end of my senior year, I received the Outstanding Migrant Senior Award. It's a huge honor that is given annually to one migrant student of the Omaha Public School system. My mom couldn't come to the ceremony, because she had to work, but my dad and siblings were there. They were very proud.

I got the scholarship! During the daytime, I attend the University of Nebraska, Omaha. I take classes like Human Relations, Human Rights, Geography, Economics. Someday, I hope to work for the United Nations.

My parents are very strict with us about religion. Every Sunday, they wake us up early to go to church. We're Baptists. They are less strict about me dating, but they always remind me that education comes first. They say, "Remember why you're here. Remember your goals. Remember what you want to do for your community and family, and then make decisions, thinking about your goals, thinking about what you want to do in life."

Mom still works at the meatpacking factory. She understands English but is so shy she doesn't speak. My younger brother and sisters came here when they were very little and are not comfortable speaking Karen. Mom understands what they say when they speak in English, but she responds in Karen. We call our language Karenglish. I sometimes think back to my days in the camp, when my greatest pleasure was playing marbles under the house. Now I come home and see my younger brother and sisters playing video games on their computers.

Nathan, at the time using his given name, Hei Blut, and his award

Nathan on campus

My dad told his tutor that he wanted to be a citizen, so he taught my dad American history. My dad learned about all the presidents, the Constitution, and how the government works. He took the test, passed, and became a citizen. Because they were all under eighteen, my siblings became citizens through my dad. My mom was working and couldn't take off time to take the test. She's not a citizen; she's a resident. Although she worries a lot about paying the bills and the mortgage, she says that she's happy now. She has had to run since she was a little kid. Now she has a real home.

By this point I was over eighteen, so I had to become a citizen separately. I took the test and passed it. I thought about all the obstacles my family overcame to come here: the language barriers, moving around to find work, adapting to a new culture, making new friends. Becoming an American citizen was a very proud moment for me. I never had citizenship in any country that I had lived in. My ethnicity is Karen, but I had never been to the Karen state in Myanmar. I was born in Thailand, but I was never a citizen of Thailand. I never had an ID, so I couldn't travel to other countries. For the first time in my life, I felt that I belonged to a country. Yes. When people from other countries ask me where I'm from, I say, "I am from America."

ETHIOPIA

⬤ DIMMA REFUGEE
CAMP

✪ ADDIS ABABA

■ JIMMA

Lake
Abaya

Lake
Chamo

Lake
Turkana

KENYA

PART III
RUN

Nyarout

COUNTRY OF ORIGIN:
South Sudan

ETHNIC GROUP:
Nuer

Nyarout

9
In Africa

When you see photographs of emaciated children whose rib cages, arms, and legs look skeletal, whose bellies are bloated, and whose huge round eyes have a faraway look, often they are children from the world's youngest nation, South Sudan. This northeastern African country has faced floods, droughts, famine, and war. Constant war.

Sixty-four ethnic tribes populate South Sudan. The largest group are the Dinkas, who live primarily in the western part of the country, followed by the Nuers, who live to the south, in the Upper Nile Valley. On July 9, 2011, when the country won its independence from Sudan, ancient tribal hostilities reemerged. As of this writing, civil war rages on. Entire villages have been burned to the ground. Many citizens have been killed. Many people have been forced to flee to refugee camps in neighboring countries. This war has no end in sight. Millions of people are on the run. There is no time to recultivate burned-out crops. Run. No time to rebuild destroyed homes. Run.

One such runner was a Nuer child named Nyarout. As a young girl, she followed the cultural traditions of her people. As a woman, she adopted the lifestyle of an independent American.

Nyarout says, "All that I hold inside me is here in this book. Now somebody like you can read my story and know about people like me, people who lived through hell. Many people like me are still living through hell. You need to know this."

When I have a bad day, a sad day, when I feel like I'm going to cry, or think I'm going to do something stupid, I go to the bathroom and look at myself in the mirror. Then I have Nyarout in the mirror and Nyarout out. Nyarout out talks to Nyarout in the mirror. I say, "Nyarout, are you stupid? Why are you sad? You can do this!" I tell the mirror Nyarout, "If you want to cry, go ahead. Get it out. Go loud. Cry it out and you will feel better." After that, I take a shower, put on my makeup, put on my clothes, and go out. I feel better.

In Africa, we didn't have to work at jobs eight hours a day. We didn't have bills to pay. We didn't have to come home from work, clean the house, cook, do the laundry, and take care of the children alone. Sometimes I feel like I want to give up on life because this is a hard life. Then I think, whaaaat? In Africa, we didn't even have clean water; we didn't even have food to eat. Here in the U.S., I work in a clean place; I come home and sleep in a good house, in a good bed. I don't have to cook with wood, because I have a real stove. Then I feel stronger. I look at my American-born kids and think about my mom, and about my family still in Africa.

NASIR, SOUTH SUDAN

I was born into a big family. My father had three wives, and each wife had six or seven kids. My mom was his youngest wife, his last wife. We lived in a village called Nasir, not far from the Ethiopian border. We lived in a large compound surrounded by a fence. Four houses were inside the compound: one house for each wife and her kids and one for my father. I slept with my mamma. The houses were made with our hands, using palm leaves. It wasn't like the houses here in Nebraska.

When a man has a lot of kids and a lot of wives, he can't provide for them alone. The wives worked to bring food to the table for the family. The wives had a nice relationship. That's why me and my siblings love one another. If you see us, you would never know that we have different mothers.

To be honest, I do not think it's right for a man to have two or three wives. A long, long time ago, when my country wasn't developed, our great-grandfathers, our grandfathers, and then our fathers needed more than one wife to help grow food, take care of the hens, and have kids. The man had to marry other women to have more kids because so many infants got sick and died. There were no hospitals to go to.

But today, in a big city, or here in the U.S., where we have everything, why does a man need a second wife? Now his wife can have ten kids, and they will all live. I believe men got addicted to having more wives. And believe me, even though they had two, three wives, they treated them all the same: when a wife is new, they treat them good; when a wife gets old, they look for another one. You know what I mean?

Our compound had a separate cookhouse outside. My mom cooked her food, my stepmoms cooked their food, and then they brought everything to one table. It wasn't a "table-table." It was a cloth set on the ground under the mango tree.

We all ate together, but we were separated by age. If you were ten years old, you ate with the other ten- or eleven-year-olds. Older people eat fast and the young people don't eat fast. If you ate with people who were not your age, you would not have enough time to put much in your stomach. That's why they separated us by age.

The Nile River was about ten minutes' walk from the house. Wives and grown daughters brought water from the river in big containers that they carried on their heads. Every morning, we'd take a cup of the water and wash our faces. Instead of a shower, we just went to the river and swam. No bathroom. We'd just go in the field. During the daytime, people were not inside the house; we sat under the mango tree, enjoying the fresh breeze. We little kids spent all day in the river, swimming and playing. When I came home, my eyes were always red. My mom said, "Don't open your eyes when you are under the water!"

"But I want to see everything," I'd tell her.

If we were sick, there was no medicine like we have here in the U.S. My father gave us some green thingy that we chewed and then spit out. I don't know the name of it, but it made us feel better. When I had a fever, my mamma wrapped me in a blanket and put me in the sun. I'd sweat and sweat and sweat. My whole body be wet. And then, after probably maybe ten minutes, I'd come out and felt better. The fever broke.

When I was little, I had a bad cough. I don't know if it be asthma or what, but I could not stop coughing. I couldn't cry, either, because crying made it worse. I coughed until I couldn't breathe, until I passed out.

My daddy tried everything to help me. He even took me to the city to get some shots and some pills. Nothing helped. I tried and tried and tried not to cough, but every time I ate something, I coughed more. I became very, very, very tiny, like all my meat was gone. I was only bones. My father called me Nyaluot, which means "tiny" in Nuer, my language.

One day, my daddy said, "Well, you know what? I'm going to kill her." He said that to us.

"What? You're going to kill me?"

"Yeah, I'm going to try something because I'm tired of this coughing."

He got a little, tiny knife, like the knife they use when you have surgery, and he said, "Lay down."

I said, "You going to cut my throat?"

"No, no, I'm not going to cut your throat. Just lay down." And then he made the older siblings hold my hands and legs. He started cutting my chest. I was crying and screaming because it hurt. There was a lot of blood. After that, every morning and every night, he took a cloth with boiling water and put it on my chest and my back. It hurt. In one week, guess what happened? I felt better. I felt good. And the cough never came back again. I asked him, "How did you imagine this? How did you know cutting is going to save me?"

He said, "Everything is about trying. You try things. If you think this is not working, try another way to do it." I'll never forget that. If you're strong, you try different things. If one doesn't work out, try something else, just like my daddy did.

ETANG REFUGEE CAMP, ETHIOPIA; NASIR, SOUTH SUDAN

I was about seven years old when the war started, too young to remember much. I remember hearing gunshots. There was lots of confusion because everybody was running. Kids got separated from their families. The lucky kids, like me, stayed with their families. We ran to a refugee camp in Ethiopia called Etang.

After two years, the Ethiopian people started fighting with themselves, so we left Etang and went back to South Sudan. Our home was destroyed, and we had to rebuild everything. We stayed in our new home for only a year because a new war started. When the second war started, I was in school with my brother Michael. Michael's the son of my father's first wife.

One day, David, my older brother from my father's second wife, came to the school and collected us. We started running, back to Ethiopia. This time I was not so lucky, I was separated from my parents. We didn't know where they were, and there was no time to look for them. Gunshots came from everywhere and from nowhere. There was dust. It was smoky; houses were burning. We ran for our lives. Gunshots don't recognize the kids. Gunshots don't recognize the older people. They hit anyone. They hit everyone.

We just ran. Many people were running beside us. Many people died. I saw them. It took many years before I could sleep at night. I'd wake up screaming or I'd jump up and start running.

As we ran, I heard David scream, "I got hit!"

He had been shot in the leg. There was blood everywhere. He shouted at us, "You guys go!"

"How we going to leave you? You're bleeding."

"You guys have to go! GO!"

We didn't know what to do. We were too young to pick him up and carry him ourselves. Some people who knew David came by, picked him up, and hid him in the bushes. Me and Michael joined the others who were running from nowhere to nowhere, just running not to die. We got to a clearing place where many people gathered. But we still didn't see our parents. We told some guys that David was shot. Around four or five hours later, after the shooting cooled down, Michael, me, and his friends went back for David. He was still alive.

The older guys picked him up and carried him to the river. They found a canoe and we all got in. We rowed to our old refugee camp, Etang. We reached Etang, but the entire camp had been destroyed. I don't know who destroyed it. We went back into the canoe and continued rowing to we don't know where. The U.N. found us, put us on a bus, and took us to a town called Gambela, in Ethiopia. From Gambela, we were moved to another refugee camp, called Dimma.

DIMMA; ADDIS ABABA, ETHIOPIA

Being a refugee is not easy. Sometimes you must go from place to place to place. There are a lot of people. Everyone is in crisis. Everyone is in trauma. The water is not that clean. Bad water kills a lot of kids and a lot of elders. We must rely on the U.N. to bring clean water, and sometimes they run out. If a sickness comes, like a cold, it goes to everybody. If a serious disease comes out, no one is safe. The sanitation is not that good. A refugee camp is not a very good place. I didn't want to be a refugee. But I was a refugee for half my whole life.

In Dimma, we were given food, we were given clothes, and we were given some money because we had left with nothing. The camp was organized in blocks — Block One, Block Two, Block Three. We were in Block Six. We lived in a tent until they could make houses. Our house looked exactly like the one we had at home, one big room made with palms. To sleep, we put plastic on the dirt floor, and then a blanket on top of the plastic. We had another blanket to cover us. It was not very comfortable. No pillows. No mattress. Oh, no.

The camp collected many lost kids [who came to be known as the Lost Boys and Girls of Sudan] and put them in a shelter. They fed them, gave them some clothes and blankets. Refugee families went to the shelter to look for their children. If a parent didn't come, the child was considered lost. The shelter area was open two times a week. The first week we went there, we didn't find anyone from our family. The second week we went there, we found Zatrak, my mother's youngest son. He was four or five — I'm not really sure how old. That was a joyful time. We were crying. We thought all the rest of our family was gone.

Zatrak was with two other young boys, who were our cousins. We took all three boys to our house in the camp, and we grew to a family of six. There was no school. No school at all. The children played all day.

The U.N. people cut [operated on] David's leg, and he got better. He started walking again. In Africa, we didn't have cars. We walked long distances to fetch things: food, water, showers, everything. And imagine, when women walk, we have a big huge container of water or grain on our head. Even though this was considered women's work, my brothers had to do it because I was too little. After a while, David's leg got swollen again. The U.N. tried cutting him again.

Sometimes there was not enough food. The food that was delivered was not cooked. The U.N. brought us dried food, like corn, then we cooked it ourselves. Oil is the only food the U.N. gave us that didn't have to be changed into something else. They brought the oil in a huge container, and then they measured cups of it to each family.

Before Dimma was built, the Ethiopian people didn't have much business. When we arrived, they had a small area near the camp where we'd take our corn and turn it into flour. They used a *taawun*. I don't know how you call this machine in English. It was a good business for them. They sold us meat and vegetables. To get the meat and vegetables, we had to sell some of the corn the U.N. gave us. If the U.N. gave us three bags of corn, we saved two and sold one. This was illegal. We were not allowed to sell things the U.N. gave us, but we had no money. How else could we get meat and fruit and vegetables? If we were caught, we could get into trouble. They could take away our refugee cards. Without that card, we'd get nothing, nothing at all.

At first, my brothers got the food and cooked because I was too young to do the women's work. Once I turned twelve, I became like the wife, like the mother. Life became too difficult because I was still so young. I woke up early in the morning, got some clean water, came back to the house, and cooked the meal. I didn't play with the kids anymore. I worked like a housewife.

To get clean water, like the water we have here in the sink, I'd wake up at four o'clock in the morning to go on the water line. Maybe I didn't get the water until ten o'clock because the line was so long. Sometimes the water would be gone, and we waited until they brought in more.

We had big plastic jugs that we carried on our heads. We carried everything on our heads. We'd wrap cloth on our heads. I don't know how you call it in English, but we call it *thath*. I took a scarf or T-shirt and I wrapped it around the top of my head to balance the heavy jug. Sometimes the jug hurt, because I was only twelve years old, and not very strong.

The morning water lasted for the day's cooking and cleaning. And then I got the evening water. Some of the people working in the water area were very nice. If you got a nice person, especially if you were a young girl, they'd let you leave a second container in the evening line. Every container had a name or something to recognize as your container. Otherwise, you would be on line all day.

There was this older girl that didn't like me for some reason. She didn't want me in the line. She threw my container away. I asked her, "Why did you do that?"

"Get out of my face." That's all she said to me.

On the first day, I let it go. And then the second day, she did it again, and I let it go. On the third day, as soon as I took my water, she came, kicked the container, and the water spilled out. I had to go back on the line to get more. And then I got mad. We fought. I was younger than she was, but I tried my best to be a fighter because I had to defend myself.

The guys who kept the line in order tried to stop the fight. They separated us, but they couldn't take us to jail because there was no jail. After that we be cool; we even became friends.

African life is not like American life. In America, if you fight with somebody, if you hurt somebody, you go to jail. In the refugee camp, if you fight with somebody, you get away with it. Maybe, if you have a family, they be mad and ask who started the fight. But if you are somebody like me, with no adult family to care about me, I had to take care of it myself. There were so many people in the camp, lots of fights broke out. My younger brother Zatrak was always fighting.

I watched the kids who had parents play. It was sad seeing kids my age playing, happy. They didn't need to care about what they were going to eat later, what they were going to eat tomorrow. Some kids enjoyed themselves and played all day, while other kids struggled. I'm one of the kids who struggled. Sometimes I cried. I missed my old life. I missed my mamma.

We wanted to know if our family was alive in a different refugee camp. You needed money to travel to other refugee camps, and we didn't have any. Besides, we were too young to travel alone. David was old enough, but he couldn't walk long distances; he couldn't go anywhere. We were stuck, but at least we were stuck together.

There were lots of lost kids, kids who didn't have any family around. They were young and didn't know how to be safe. They didn't know if they be alive tomorrow, or if they be dead tomorrow, you know? Some people had a good heart. They took care of those lost kids. They brought them to their house and treated them like their own children. There was a woman from my block that we'd go to for help. She took care of us sometimes. She was married with her own children, but she helped me do things, things that I didn't know how to do, things that I couldn't do because I was not yet a woman. She took care of us even though we never knew her back in Sudan. She just felt sorry for us and tried to help.

I remembered my mom as a very strong woman. I remembered her working in the field, like people here who work on a farm. I remembered how proud she was. I thought, okay, even though I'm young, if she did that, I can do it.

In 1996, when I was fifteen, David's leg got worse. The U.N. sent him to Addis Ababa, the capital city of Ethiopia. At the hospital, the doctors separated his leg from his body. I went to Addis Ababa to help him. We stayed in a room near the hospital, and I became like a wife. I washed his clothes and cooked. My other brothers stayed in the refugee camp while me and David lived in Addis Ababa. During that time, we put our names on a list to immigrate to the United States. I wanted to go to the U.S. so much because I heard that it was a safe place. I heard that people who had already gone to the U.S. could support their families and not rely on the U.N. I thought that if I went to U.S., I could take care of my family.

While we were living in Addis Ababa, David met a girl who someone thought would be a good wife for him. I knew for sure she was never going to be a good wife, because she acted weird. But I couldn't speak bad about her because I didn't want my brother to feel bad.

SHERKOLE, ADDIS ABABA

In 1998, the Ethiopian government collected all the Sudanese people who were staying in Addis Ababa and took us to a new refugee camp called Sherkole. David, his wife, and I lived in a tent until we could make a house with wood. Soon Michael, Zatrak, and our cousins moved in too. There was still no school. The children played all day.

By now, I was seventeen years old and didn't want to play with kids. Doing things by myself became easier. I acted like a woman. That means I prepared everything, carried the water, shopped for food. I'd go to the market to sell some of the sorghum the U.N. gave us for meat and honey. I learned to say, "I'll give you this; you give me that."

When we first moved to Sherkole, David's wife was okay. She helped him get used to the fake leg that they gave him in the hospital. She walked with him and did his laundry. But that's all she did. I did everything else: bring the water for him to shower, cook, clean, get his medicines. All day, I did this and I did that. She just watched. She was a weird woman.

David started going to the Presbyterian church in the refugee camp. He became one of the church leaders, and then an evangelist minister. Guests came to our house all the time. I thought to myself, he has a wife; she can do the things that I do. And guess what? She just kept sitting down, making herself clean, and doing things that she's not supposed to do, girlie things, like putting on her nail polish and combing her hair. Finally I told her, "Hey, I'm not the wife in this house. You're wife! You can do the things that I do. I'll show you how; you can do this." She didn't care. She continued to act just like a guest. She be sitting there, watching me work. When the food was ready, she came and ate.

Sometimes I felt like I didn't want to let her eat. I kept my mouth quiet. If my brother wanted it that way, I had no choice. I was not going to tell him not to be with this lady. My little brother Zatrak didn't like her at all. He told me, "Nyarout, I want to beat up this lady." "Come on, don't do that. Don't do that," I'd tell him. "Just leave it."

In Sherkole, we became lucky. David got a notice to come for an interview to go to the U.S. He'd been on the waiting list for two years since we were in Dimma. The two lost boys, our cousins, were still living with us. David said, "I can't leave them. Let's try to take them with us."

Everyone who lived with us could go to the United States, including our cousins. But first we must all be interviewed and checked out. The interview was hard. They asked the same things, again and again. "How did the war start?" "How did you get to here?" "How many days did it take to go from Nasir to Ethiopia?" Sometimes they asked the same question in a different way. I guess it was to check that we were honest. One question hurt us the most: "Where are the other family members, like your father and mother?" That question hurt us because, at this point, we didn't know where our parents were. Were they okay? Were they alive? We had no idea. We went through many interviews, we answered many questions, we had many medical checkups, and we passed everything.

Months later — I'm not sure how many months — we found out that our parents were alive in Ethiopia too, in another refugee camp.

ONE FINE DAY

My brother and I left the Sherkole refugee camp to go to Addis Ababa for our orientation meeting. Orientation is the last step before coming to the U.S. In the morning, like, nine in the morning, we were on the way to the meeting. We saw a friend from the camp — his name is Both — who was also visiting Addis Ababa. He came up to us in the street and said, "Your mom is here."

Both is a good guy. We were good friends. I said to him, "Please, don't lie to us." I wanted to see my parents so bad before I left. "No, I'm not lying." And then he said, "I can take you over there where she at."

When I saw my mom, I was so happy I didn't even feel myself. I couldn't even look at her. I cried and cried and cried happiness tears. I was crying very loud — like really, really loud. I couldn't believe it was her. My mom was crying too. She said, "I can't even believe how much you've grown." It had been seven years since I'd seen her. That's a long time for a child.

Mom had heard that we were in Addis Ababa. She had enough money to buy one bus ticket to come and try to find us. Refugees don't have phones. We don't have the Internet. To find one another, we ask people who are traveling from one camp to another if a family member is in the camp. Sometimes we give the traveler letters in the hope that the person meets our family. My mom asked every Sudanese she saw if they knew about us. And then that guy, Both, told her, "Yeah, I know them. They in Sherkole."

Later, when we got to the orientation meeting, they told us about the life and the rules in the U.S. They said that we will have the freedom to do whatever we wanted to do, except killing and stealing. They taught us that if you became a criminal, if you did some bad stuff, they would deport you back to where you came from. I worried about Zatrak, my younger brother. He was a fighter. He was always getting into fights.

They said that you could have a job if you were old enough, like eighteen and up. They said that when you earn your money, it's your money.

After our orientation, me and David went back to the refugee camp. We left my mom in Addis Ababa. It wasn't hard to say goodbye, because we knew that we were coming back. The hard time to say goodbye was when we left to come over here. My mom couldn't come with us because she needed a form to come over here. Our process was already done but hers wasn't. She stayed in Africa.

Before we left, we had four more days to be with our mom in Addis Ababa. The U.N. gave us some money, so we rented a house rather than stay in a hotel. It was me, my brothers, my mom, and David's wife. The only person missing for me was my dad. He was in another refugee camp somewhere. I remember the things that we used to do because I was Daddy's little girl, his tiny, skinny Nyaluot. I never saw my father again. I can't even remember his face.

My mom told me that she and my father had arranged a marriage for me in the U.S. They didn't know the guy; they knew his family. He was the father of Both, my friend who had found my mother in Addis Ababa. Since my dad was not coming to the U.S. with us, David, the oldest son, was in charge to make this happen. I didn't say nothing. I just kept quiet, because if I said no, they would still make me do it. But I started to worry about what life in the U.S. had in store for me.

10
In America

TENNESSEE

On August 11, 1999, we flew to America. The flight was very scary. It was weird to be in the plane. The food was different. My younger brother, he opened a wrapper and looked at some brown thing. David opened one too and put it in his mouth. He immediately took it out and gave it to me. He said, "Try this — it's really, really good."

"Okay, what is it?"

"Just eat it. It's good! Try it." And then when I put it in my mouth, it was very nasty. I spit it out, I didn't like it. We didn't have chocolate in our country.

We landed in New York City. There were these huge screens that were so clean you can see yourself. You couldn't walk through them, though. We never saw glass so big. Oh, my gosh, it was weird.

There were lots of people in the airport. I had never seen fat people before, and I was scared to see people so big. I stared at them. Seriously? People can get fat like that? In my country, people are so skinny. How did they get so much food to be fat like that?

I didn't understand what anybody was saying. I speak Nuer and a little Ethiopian. This new language, English, was confusing.

We walked around the airport with plastic cards on our backs that said we were refugees. At one point, a girl, a stranger, came up to me and wanted to hug me. She wanted to welcome me, but because I didn't speak English, I didn't understand what she was trying to do. She scared me.

We had our I-94, a document that said we could come to the U.S. That's a document that you use to get your Social Security, to get your ID, and all these things. That's the only document they gave us in Addis Ababa.

We changed planes to go to Nashville, Tennessee, our new home in the U.S. It was my younger brother Zatrak, Michael, David, his wife, the two cousins, and me. At the Nashville airport, we met the people who sponsored us, friends from the camp who had already settled in Nashville, and the man my parents had arranged for me to marry. He was just standing there, with a flower in his hand. He was too old for me. He was, like, fifty years old, and I was eighteen. No, I did not like him. I did not like him at all. I grabbed the flower and walked away. I didn't even shake his hand.

One of my friends from the refugee camp was at the airport too. I hadn't seen her for a year. We hugged and cried. My friend said, "Why don't you give him a hug?"

"I don't know him." We just left in the car. That was it. I didn't say anything to him at the airport.

Our sponsors took us to a huge apartment with five bedrooms. We didn't have big apartments in Africa, we only had the small houses, so this was totally different. The sponsor taught us how to use the stove and things. We were living with regular people, not with other refugees. It was amazing there.

In Africa, everything be outside. In Nashville, Tennessee, everything be inside. The bathroom be inside. The kitchen be inside. The garbage cans be inside. The shower be inside. The shower! The shower was good. In Addis Ababa, we just got some water on your hand and put it on your body. Oh, I liked showers immediately. Yes, yes, yes.

Life in the U.S. was simple but not simple. Little things were big things. I couldn't drink the water in the refrigerator. It made my teeth feel funny. Yeah, cold. Ice cream was sweet, but too cold. And it melted, so it was messy. No, I didn't like ice cream.

Soon after we arrived in Tennessee, David's wife left him and moved to Seattle. I had the feeling that something like that would happen. I told David that I didn't like her in the first place. I said, "I just didn't want to hurt your feelings, so couldn't speak up about her."

At the orientation meeting back in Addis Ababa, I learned that the United States is a free country, and you can do whatever you want, and you can say whatever you want. So I said to David, "No, I won't marry this man."

David was furious. On the one side, he loved me and wanted me to be happy. On the other side, as the firstborn son in the family, it was his job to carry out the commands of our father; it was his job to preserve the traditions of our culture. So when I said I wouldn't marry this old man, trouble started in our family. David and my brothers wouldn't talk to me. The man had already paid David six thousand dollars to marry me. I told David that I would pay him back. David was so angry, he made me leave the apartment. Because I was set to be in an arranged marriage with this guy, I had to go to his house. My little brother Zatrak wanted to come with me, and I took him because I felt that he could protect me. We moved to a small city called Gallatin, about thirty miles northeast of Nashville. It wasn't a happy home, because I didn't like the guy. We weren't legally married in an American way; we were married in our culture way. He forced me for sex. It was awful. I was a virgin. I told him I'm unhappy. I told him, "I do not love you. I am never going to love you.

We're never going to happen. I will find a way to leave you, but now, because I have nowhere to go, I'm staying here."

Sometimes I felt like I wanted to kill myself because I didn't have nowhere to go. My brother David didn't want me to live with him. David cared about how I felt, but after our father decided on this marriage, there was nothing he could do. It wasn't his idea for me to get married with that guy. The other relatives who had already moved to the U.S. didn't want me either. They couldn't go against my father's decision, because arranged marriages are part of our culture. The deal was done and that was the end of that.

My "husband" wanted me to get pregnant. He had sex with me anytime he wanted. I didn't know nothing about birth control, but it didn't matter, I didn't get pregnant. He said that something was wrong with me, that I couldn't have kids. He took me to a doctor, then another doctor, then another doctor. I didn't know what the doctor said because I didn't speak English. My husband told me that the doctor said, "Something's going on in your stomach or whatever." I thought, okay, if something's wrong with me, why can't they give me medicine to treat that?

"Well, I have my period regularly, every month. I never miss it since my first period. If my period comes, I don't have problems. I never complain. It's just regular." I'd have cramps, but not that bad cramps. "Any girl, any woman, can have a baby," he said to me. "Something's wrong."

To be honest with you, he was not a bad guy. He was a nice guy, but the problem was I wasn't in love with him. He cared about me, even when I said bad things to him. He never treated me bad, like, hit me or nothing. No, he never did that. He was in love with me. If I didn't eat, he didn't eat. But the problem was the sex.

I met a translator who went to the doctor with me while I had my period. The doctor said to the translator, "She's very active. She can have a kid. There's nothing wrong with her." This was when I decided that I must leave. Now that the guy knew I can have kids, he would abuse me, by having sex, a lot more.

Two months later, I told him that I wanted to get a job, I wanted to go to school, and I wanted to learn English. In the camps, I never had the chance to get an education. But the guy didn't want me to go to school. I think he didn't want me to learn. He was okay about me getting a job; he would like the extra money, right? He took me to the company where he worked. He helped me fill out the application. Then they called me for an interview. I had the interview and got a job making glass for windows.

There was an older white lady named Elizabeth who worked with me. She knew that something was wrong. One day she asked me. "Nyarout, do you love that guy?" I don't remember how we communicated, because I still didn't speak English. I think we used sign language.

I said, "Yeah."

"No. No, you don't."

"Wow. How you know this?"

"Well, because you're too young for him."

I was very, very tiny, you know? I didn't even look eighteen. I looked maybe fifteen because I was skinny.

I said, "I know." I really don't remember how I communicated this.

Elizabeth was American. Every time I came to work, she patted my shoulder. Yup, every time she saw me, pat, pat, pat. She was an older lady. I think she was probably maybe fifty or forty-something.

Another one of these ladies, who was African American, lived next door. I told her my problem. I told her what was going on. Again, I didn't know how she understood me, but I told her that I was not happy, and she understood.

"I will help you."

"How are you going to help me?"

"I'm going to find you a place to go, I'm going to find a good shelter for you. You don't speak English. I don't want you in a public shelter, because I want you to be safe and I want you to be taken care of."

Two weeks later, she asked me three times, "Nyarout, do you want to get out of here?"

And three times I said, "Yes."

The guy had all my documents. He had my Social Security [card]. He had my I-94. I searched the house for them. When I found my documents, I told the neighbor that I could go the next morning. I told her that when the guy goes to school, she could come and take me. (I don't know what kind of school he went to.)

The day before I left, I got my paycheck. I wanted to keep my paycheck because I didn't know where I was going, and that was all the money I had. Usually, when I got a paycheck, I gave it to him.

This day he didn't want to go to school. I tried something different to get him out of the house. I dumped the orange juice in the refrigerator into the sink. "Oh, we run out of juice," I told him. "Go to the store and buy some juice."

He said, "Okay, but give me your check and I'll take it to the bank."

"I don't want you to take it to the bank. We'll go to the bank together. I want to buy something." He told me, no, he wanted the money in the bank. "Okay, here!" I gave him the check just so he would leave.

Right after he left, I knocked on the lady's door. I left the house empty, with no money. I ran. I later heard that Zatrak stayed in the house for a while. When he realized I wasn't coming back, he moved back to David's house.

In my country, if you divorce a husband, the family gets a bad credit [reputation]. My family wanted everything to be perfect. Well, you know, everything is not always perfect. There's always something that you're not going to like, and there's always something you're going to walk away from. But my people, all they care about is a good credit, a good credit, a good credit. That's why me and David started disagreeing about things. Probably because he's older, he holds on to the old ways. When David found out I left this man, he didn't want to talk to me. He said that I was going against the wishes of my mother and father, against my culture. I was the first person to give our family bad credit.

From 2000 to 2008, David did not talk to me the way we used to talk. He still called to see that I was okay, but he said things like, "Nyarout, how you guys doing? Good?" That's it. No real talk.

The shelter was in a very nice three-bedroom house. There were two other women staying there, one from India and a Mexican lady with two kids. Kimberly, the head of the shelter, was very, very nice. She bought our clothes, she bought our food, she bought everything that we needed. She was an American, a white lady. We each had our own place in the refrigerator for our food.

The Mexican lady was mean to me. She made up things: "Nyarout did this, Nyarout did that. Nyarout doesn't do the dishes. Nyarout eats our food." That was not true. But because I didn't speak English, I could not defend myself with the truth.

Kimberly talked to me about eating the lady's food. I didn't understand; I didn't understand nothing. I started crying and crying. Kimberly talked to me like I was deaf, loud, and using body language. I was crying so hard. I wished I could just speak English so I could tell her the truth.

The other girl at the shelter, the Indian girl, was pregnant. One day, when she came back from her doctor's appointment, the owner asked her, "Do you know if Nyarout is eating the other people's food?" The Indian girl walked to the refrigerator, opened it, and showed Kimberly that we each had our own food. "Why would Nyarout eat our food when she has her own right here?"

Kimberly came to me, hugged me, and tried to comfort me. She took me away to her own house. Her own house!

My first winter in Tennessee was in Kimberly's house. One day, one of my friends from the camp called and said, "Nyarout, open the window." I opened the window and asked, "What is that white thing?"

She said, "Open the door and go out."

I had the phone on my ear. She said, "Don't put your shoes on — just walk."

"Oh, my goodness. Is this a sand or something?"

"Just feel it." I was jumping on it. It felt so cold. "What is this thing?"

"It's snow."

"Oh, snow." I didn't know what that was. I knew that it was good, but cold, really, cold. Snow was good here in America, but it would not be good in Africa. Here we have jackets and boots and gloves. We have heat in the house. We didn't have those things in Africa.

After six months, I learned that one of my cousins was living in Jacksonville, Florida. I told Kimberly I was going to live with my cousin. She said, "I don't know if you're going to be safe there, because you don't speak enough English yet." She worried.

I said, "She's my cousin, she's married, she has a kid. I'll be fine."

Kimberly bought me a ticket to Florida.

JACKSONVILLE, FLORIDA

In Florida, I got a dishwashing job in a kitchen at Jacksonville University. Eventually I was able to save enough money to send my husband the six thousand dollars he paid my family to marry me. The warm weather and thick, leafy bushes reminded me of home. Most nights I was having bad dreams about bombs, guns, and burning buildings. Then, the night of July 4, something terrible happened. I heard sounds that sounded like guns. "NO! NO! IT'S NOT HAPPENING AGAIN!" I ran to my cousin. "Let's go!"

"Where are we going?"

"It is happening again! Here in America!" Her husband thought my fear was funny. But my cousin yelled at him, "No, this is not funny." Her husband stopped laughing and held my hand and hugged me. He took me outside to see the beautiful colors in the sky. "See? Look at the sky. See the beautiful colors? This is what happens on Independence Day, the day when we became an independent country. You will see this every year."

Now I'm okay about fireworks. I even go to see them. But I'm still scared of guns. When I see anybody with a gun, that scares me.

In Florida, I met Bol. Bol was from South Sudan too, but from a different village. We spoke the same language. I was attracted to him, but I wasn't in love with him.

My family still didn't want me, so I thought, why can't I have my own family? I can make my own family. Maybe that would make me happy. My ex-husband's words that I couldn't have kids stuck in my mind. My ex-husband's actions made me scared to love. I wanted to have sex with Bol to see if I could get pregnant.

I got pregnant right away. After I found out that I was pregnant, I told Bol, "I'm not going to be with you." I was happy to be here in the U.S., but I was not happy to live with a man because of what I had experienced, you know? I didn't believe that Bol cared enough about me, loved me, the way I needed to be loved. I left. Yes, I left. That may seem hard, but I needed to find my own way in the world. I moved to Salt Lake City, Utah, because my uncle, my mom's brother, invited me to live with them so his wife could help me with the child.

UTAH

In Salt Lake City, I started ESL [English as a Second Language] courses to learn English. I wasn't a full-time student, but at least this was a start. Until now, I had had no schooling but for the year before the war. I couldn't even read my own language.

Bol followed me to Salt Lake City. He wanted to be with me for the birth of our child. "I want to be with you. I want to help you take care of the child. I want to be into your life." He even talked to my family back in Africa.

By this point, one of my dad's wives had died, and the rest of the family left the refugee camp and moved to Gambela, in Ethiopia. Bol's father had left his small town and moved to Gambela too. We Sudanese people, Nuer people, always give a person a place to stay. Even if that person is not a relative, our door is open. Bol's father had knocked on my parents' door in Addis Ababa and stayed. Was this a coincidence or was it fate? I'll never know the answer to that question.

Bol called his dad and said, "I got a girl pregnant and I want to marry her."

"Who is that?" his father asked.

Bol said my name and my father's name and my grandfather's name.

Bol's father said, "Oh, I'm living in their house."

Bol talked to my mom. He said, "I want to be with Nyarout. I want to marry her." Then he said, "Ask Nyarout's father how many cows he wants, and I will give them to him." Bol would not actually send a cow; he would send money to buy a cow. In our culture, women cannot talk about a girl's marriage. Men made those arrangements. But my father was not home.

Then Bol called to me, "Hey, your mamma wants to talk to you. She's in Gambela."

"How do you know that my mom is in Gambela?" My mom had stopped talking to me when I left my husband. Right then and there, Bol made peace for me with my mom. When I spoke to her, she told me, "Your boyfriend says he wants to marry you, and all this." I said, "Well, I am not planning to marry him, because I don't know if you will approve my marriage. You won't talk to me. You guys made David throw me out."

"Nyarout, I didn't have a choice. You know that whatever your father says, I must go with it, even though I love you very much. When it comes to marriage, I can't make that choice for you. My only choice was to give life to you."

"What kind of life did you give me?" I snapped at her. "If I was in Africa, and you made me marry that guy, I would kill myself because I don't want him at all. So in the end, there would be no life."

"Well," she said, "I don't know. I don't know. I don't know what to do. Your father decides everything."

Bol sent my mom five hundred dollars. He said, "This is not for marriage; it is a gift for you."

In Salt Lake City, I had my first daughter, Nyagoa. The love I felt for her . . . I don't know how to explain it. It was greater than anything I had imagined. In the days that followed, I couldn't stop thinking about my own mother. I called her in Gambela to apologize. "I'm sorry for everything I said to you." She told me that I didn't have to apologize. She told me that she would always love me. This is the love that mothers share with their children. This is the love that I now had with my own daughter.

Even though I felt so much love for Nyagoa, I knew nothing about being a mother. My uncle's wife helped me. When my daughter cried at night, she woke up to take care of her. I slept through the night.

Nyarout, Bol, and their daughter, Nyagoa, moved to Denison, Iowa, where Bol found a job in the meatpacking industry.

DENISON, IOWA

At age twenty, I finally started going to school through Job Corps. I took more ESL classes and my English got better — not too much better.

Two years later, in 2002, when I was twenty-two years old, maybe twenty-one, my second daughter, Nyabima, was born. Bol and I were living together, but we were not married. Bol worked in the morning, I went to school in the morning, and the girls went to day care. I asked Bol to work a second shift while I was in school. He didn't want to work a second shift. I got a job just to pay for child care so that I could go to school. I found a job packing bacon at a meat company. I started work at three thirty in the afternoon and did a twelve-hour shift, six days a week. I went to school in the morning. There was no time to sleep.

At the meat company, you worked on probation for ninety days. After the ninety days, you got a permanent job with benefits. When I was close to my ninety days, my supervisor called me into her office and asked for my ID.

"Why?" She told me that she didn't want me to work for them anymore.

"I need to know the reason. I've been working three months. I'm never late. I never missed a day. Every time I learn one job, you send me to a different job. And I do a good job on each one. I want to know the reason why I'm fired."

"Just give me the damn ID."

"I'm not going to give it you. I'm not going nowhere."

She lied and said that the supervisor I was working under told her that I had a mental problem.

"Have I ever had a problem with anyone at work?"

"I don't care. Just give me the damn ID."

"Okay." I threw down the ID. Then guards walked me to my locker like I had done something really bad. After I took out all my stuff, they walked me to the parking lot and waited till I left.

When I moved to America, I learned that I had rights. I decided to see if this was true. The next day, I found myself a lawyer and told him what happened. He sent me to the doctor to check if I had a mental problem. I didn't. Then we went to the court and I sued the company. The manager never showed up. She was lying. I proved that I didn't have no mental problem. And the company had to pay me. This is a good country.

Through Job Corps, I was able to get a Certified Assistant Nursing degree, and I went to work at a nursing home, taking care of elderly people. It was a very good job. But even though I was working full-time at the nursing home, day care for two girls didn't leave me with much money. One of my friends lived in Minnesota. She

Nyarout in Lincoln, Nebraska

told me that in Minnesota they helped with day care and school. I still couldn't read English good. (I can now. Now I can read books and everything in English.) I told Bol that we had to move to Minnesota. "If I can have a chance to go to school, I have to go to Minnesota."

"Okay, you and the kids can go. I'll stay here and work." That's what Bol told me.

MINNESOTA

I loved Minnesota. That's my favorite state. In the winter, it's cold, and it snowed a lot, but they did a good job clearing the roads. I moved with my kids and stayed in my friend's house. I got a job right away, packing frozen food. Soon after I started work, I applied for my own apartment. Bol followed us to Minnesota. Things were good.

The next year, I went back to Tennessee to visit Kimberly, the shelter lady who had been so kind to me. My brother Michael, who still lived in Tennessee, had softened towards me. He waited in a car with my kids while I knocked on Kimberly's office door.

When she opened it, I gave her a big hug.

She was, like, "Can I help you?" She didn't recognize me.

"Did you know a girl who used to live in your shelter? Nyarout?"

"Yeah, that little girl. She left a long time ago, I don't even know if she's okay. She never writes letters; she never calls. Is something going on with her?"

"No, nothing's going on with her. She's the one who's talking to you *right now*."

"No, no, get out of here!" She stared at me, patting my back, "Look at you! Oh, my God, now you're so big. You've grown; you've gained weight."

"Yeah, I'm growing."

I told Kimberly that when I left her, I couldn't say thank you for all that she did for me because I didn't speak enough English. I didn't have a voice to say it. "I wanted to come back because now I can speak English; now I can properly thank you." She was crying, and I was crying. When I left Tennessee for Florida, Kimberly had given me two dolls. I said, "Do you remember the two dolls that you gave me?"

"Yeah."

"They've become real."

"What are you talking about?"

"I have two daughters," and then I called to my brother to bring my daughters to us. Kimberly cried while hugging my girls.

I was so happy that I could tell Kimberly how much I appreciated what she had done for me.

In 2007, I finally got my high-school diploma. I was proud. I had a diploma, a job, and two daughters. I was working at another nursing home when I became pregnant again. That's when my son, Emanuel, was born.

The only problem was Bol. Bol loved holding on to money. He paid all the household bills, using both our salaries, but he would not give me extra cash. There were times when I didn't have enough money to buy something to eat where I worked. Things were going from bad to worse with us.

My Florida cousin had moved to Omaha, Nebraska, and my brother David was living in Lincoln, Nebraska. I told my cousin I wanted to talk with David. I wanted to make peace with him. My cousin set up a meeting between us in her house.

I went to Nebraska and told David how I felt. "I don't hate you for what happened, because it wasn't your fault I had to marry that guy. You just wanted to follow the rule that our parents made. But what I needed from you, what made me angry, was that you kicked me out. You said, 'If you don't go to that guy's house, you're not going to live with me.' That's what you said. Being angry with you is not going to gain anything. I forgive you. You lost your leg saving my life. You brought me to this beautiful country. Here, if I get sick, I get treatment. I live in a good house. I have a job. I have a car. In Africa, I never had a job so that I could buy a car. I never even rode in a car. All that I have is because of you." Then we started talking, really talking, again.

But my family back in Africa still didn't talk to me much because they felt I had left my culture. In Africa, a woman doesn't make her own choices. Here in the U.S., it's different. I decided that, because I live in America, I can make my own choices. I couldn't stay with a guy who I wasn't in love with, you know? That's why I made my own decision to be independent, to follow U.S. culture, not African culture.

I returned to Minnesota and broke up with Bol. I was taking care of three kids and working at the nursing home. I had to support my family here and also send money to my family back home.

That same year, 2007, I met Megho. He was from South Sudan but from a different tribe, the Anuak. We spoke different languages, so we communicated in English. We met because his niece and nephew were going to the same school as me. I was struggling with the ignition in my car. To fix the car cost two thousand dollars. At this time, I had no extra money to pay for the car repair. My kids were in day care or school. We had to walk to get there. It was in wintertime. Megho stepped up to help. He said, "Even though you don't want to date me, I can still help you."

He drove my son to day care and he drove my girls to school. After school, he picked me up, picked them up, dropped us off home. He was really nice.

After a while, I accepted him. He lived in his house, and I lived in my house, but he helped me with the kids. He helped me pay my bills. Sometimes he even sent money to my family back home. He treated my kids like they were his own kids. He was the best father ever. He wanted to have a child with me. I didn't agree, because I was scared.

We were together for about two years before I got pregnant. That's when I fell in love with him.

When I was four months pregnant, Megho went back to Africa to visit his family. When he returned — this was in 2009 — he changed. He became weird. He'd get mad at me really quick. I couldn't understand why he changed so much. Finally he said, "I don't want to confuse you. I found myself another girl, an Anuak girl."

He moved the girl from Austin to Minneapolis, to the same apartment building that I lived in. I lived in the first floor, and the girl lived on the third floor. Then they moved in together. At that time, I was seven months pregnant.

That's when I started talking to Nyarout in the mirror. "Take it easy. You can't have stress right now. Don't think about it."

When the contractions came, I called Megho to take me to the hospital. He was kind. He stayed with me while my baby girl, Ajeal, was being born. During the delivery, I had had an epidural in my back, and my right leg went numb. I couldn't feel my leg at all. I couldn't do anything. When I came home, Megho didn't want to help me, even though I couldn't walk. He had that woman upstairs, and she was all he cared about. I was so stressed.

One of my best friends — she lives in Omaha right now — lived in the same apartment building as me. She's like a sister to me. She helped me with the kids while I couldn't walk. She worked in the morning, came back, cooked for me, cleaned the house for me, and took care of the kids. For three months, I had nobody except this friend. My older brother David was now living in Lincoln, Nebraska, but he couldn't come and help me, because, well, he is a man, you know?

The very good thing about Minnesota is that the kids had a free school bus that picked them up in the morning and brought them home at night. I didn't have to worry about that. After three months of physical therapy, my leg got better and I started walking.

Back when I was fake-married to the old guy, I went to a party and met a big man who had lots of muscles and a long beard. His name was Mai. He looked more African American than African. I couldn't lay eyes on him directly because I was married. There was no way. But I thought about him a lot. After so many years, and four kids, I saw Mai again when I visited my family in Nebraska. (He had since moved there.) We became friends. Then we became close friends.

Mai said, "Here in Minnesota, you don't know anybody; you don't have family, only one friend. It's better that you move to Nebraska." I moved to Nebraska to be with him.

LINCOLN, NEBRASKA

Mai and I were together from 2010 to 2016. I had my last baby with him, my son Bukjiok. I loved Mai. I still do. But he's not able to make a lasting commitment. I was now a grown-up woman, right? Two of my kids were already teenagers. I was getting old. I didn't want to run around with men. I wanted my kids to see me committed to a man I could marry. Mai was not capable of marrying me. He said he loved me, he even said he wanted to marry me, but he didn't know when. For seven years I thought, maybe he's gonna change, maybe he's gonna change, maybe he's gonna change. But he didn't change.

After my son Bukjiok was born, I talked to Nyarout in the mirror again. "Why is he here? He takes no responsibility, even for his own son." After I talked to Nyarout in the mirror, I totally blocked my heart. I saw a lot of things that I couldn't see before. I felt really bad about my life. I felt terrible.

I told Mai, "I thought we could be better people together. I thought we could be a couple. I thought we could be a family. But I feel like you are not willing to be a stable man. You're not helping me." I told him to leave.

And he left.

In 2014, I went. Back to Africa to see my mom, my other brothers and sisters who had stayed behind. By now, my brothers and sisters all had kids of their own. I never did get to see my father. The civil war was going on, and my father was away. I think he was working as an adviser to the military.

My grandmother wanted to see me, but she was afraid to leave her village. She said that she wanted to hold me one more time before she died—I think she was ninety-eight years old. She said, "I don't want to die before I see you. I'm going to wait until you come." I went to her village in Ethiopia. She could only see me with one eye; she had cataracts. "I can't believe that you're here. You're here." She cried and hugged me and hugged me. When I stood up, she said, "I'm not done. I don't have enough of you." And she hugged me some more. "I don't want you to go back."

"But what about my kids? I have kids over there. If I didn't have kids, I would stay."

"Okay, I will give you many blessings that you will have many, many kids."

"Don't bless me with more children; bless me with more money."

In Africa, I realized how much I had changed. Of course, I'm still an African person, but my life is so different now. The food they eat doesn't taste good to me anymore. I can't sleep on the ground anymore. I tried it, but my back hurt so much. My African family walks long distances. I'm used to driving everywhere, not walking. And, most important, I say and do what I think, not what others tell me to think. I still love my culture. I love my people. But I love my American independence too. I would say I've become a Sudanese American.

With the money I made in America, I could build my family a house in Gambela. If I had stayed in Africa and had an arranged marriage, I probably wouldn't have been able to build my parents a house. In Africa, a married woman pretty much stays in her husband's home. I'd have to cook and do everything for my husband's parents, not my own parents. But because I'm in America and I'm not married, I can make my own way and help my own parents.

Me and my kids have a very good relationship. I tell them about the things I went through, but I encourage them not to be stressed by it. "I have you guys and that's all that matters." I tell them that we live in a country where they can go to school, have a good job, buy a beautiful house. It's up to them. I live paycheck to paycheck, but I'm doing it for them. I do not want their life to be a struggle like my life was. They listen to me. They do good in school. They do outside activities.

Nyarout holding photographs of herself with her grandmother
and mother

Nyagoa plays in a marching band, and Nyabima plays basketball and is a cheerleader. Everyone is doing pretty good.

I'm a supervisor for the all-night shift for custodial services at UNL [University of Nebraska, Lincoln]. I supervise the staff as they clean the classrooms. If I'm bored, or think I could fall asleep, I clean too. The university doesn't pay good, but it provides good benefits. My children will be able to go to the University of Nebraska, and that means so much to me. On my off days, I'm a cashier at a gas station. I still advise myself in the mirror. My life has been a struggle, yes; I'm still struggling, yes, but I'm happy.

And David? David had moved to Africa for five years. When he came back, he moved into my house. He is a pastor at our church. He also drives a taxi to help with expenses. Before he moved in, I'd come back from work, take the kids to school, sleep from ten to about two o'clock, and pick up the kids from school. I could only sleep three or four hours a day. After David came back, I was able to sleep till four in the afternoon. I drive the kids to school in the morning and David picks them up after school.

When David was in Africa, he left his car at my house. The kids would say, "Mom, is this your car?"

"No, it's Uncle David's car." That's how they knew that they had an Uncle David. But the little ones didn't remember him, because they were so young when he left. The little ones always called the car "Uncle David Car."

When David returned, they said, "Uncle David? You are real? We thought you were a car."

David and I are very close again. We've been through great changes and came out all right. But when David moved in, I told him, "You live in my house now. I'm in charge."

Nyarout and David

Nyarout and her children: Nyagoa, Emanuel, Nyabima, Ajeal, and Bukjiok

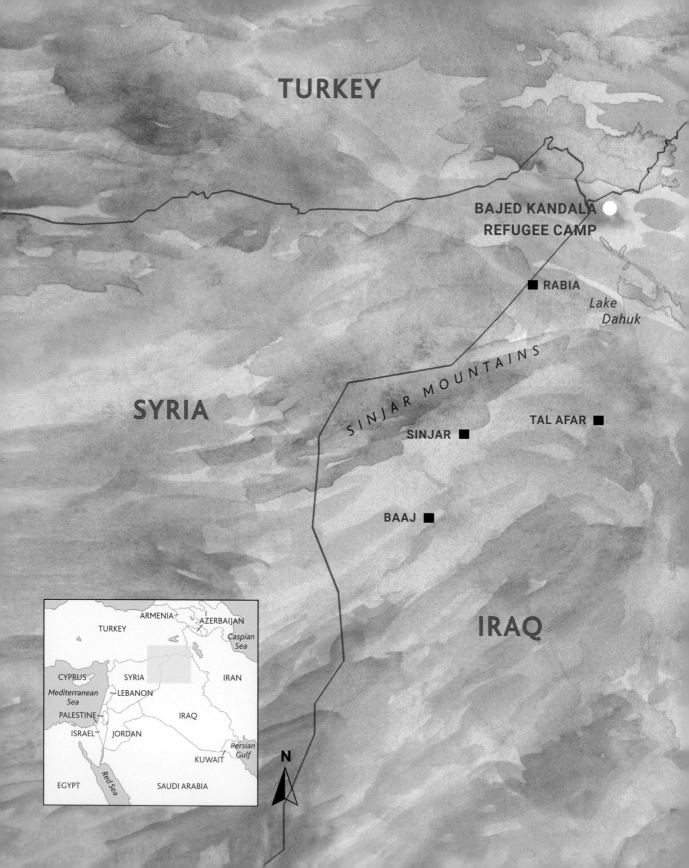

TURKEY

BAJED KANDALA
REFUGEE CAMP

■ RABIA

Lake Dahuk

S I N J A R   M O U N T A I N S

SYRIA

SINJAR ■

TAL AFAR ■

BAAJ ■

IRAQ

ARMENIA
TURKEY   AZERBAIJAN
                         Caspian Sea
CYPRUS   SYRIA   IRAN
Mediterranean Sea   LEBANON
PALESTINE   IRAQ
ISRAEL   JORDAN
                    Persian Gulf
                    KUWAIT
EGYPT   *Red Sea*   SAUDI ARABIA

N

PART IV
SURVIVE

Shireen

COUNTRY OF ORIGIN:
Northern Iraq

ETHNIC GROUP:
Yazidi

Shireen

11
Captured

In the previous chapter, Nyarout, who has lived in the United States for many years, is able to describe how she changed from an African girl to a South Sudanese American woman. Meet Shireen. Shireen has lived in Lincoln, Nebraska, for only three months and has not yet had time to adjust to a new way of life. She is still struggling to cope with the enormous brutality inflicted on her and her family. All the other participants in this book were resettled along with family members. Shireen came alone. Shireen is Yazidi.

The Yazidis (also known as Yezidi or Êzidî) are an independent ethnic society that mostly inhabited the Sinjar region in Northern Iraq. Throughout their long and fabled history, they have survived seventy-three genocides. Theirs is an ancient religion, spread orally by holy men, that is related to

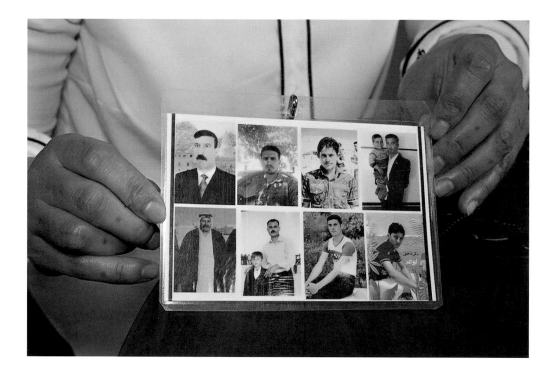

Ten of Shireen's missing family members (top row, left to right): Rasho Ibrahim, Ali Jardo, Nazar Khudeda, Hadi Jardo and his son Delhat Hadi; (bottom row, left to right): Aato Ibrahim, Khudeda Ibrahim and his son Ayman Khudeda, Khairy Aato, and Dakhil Jardo

Zoroastrianism, Mithraism, Judaism, Christianity, and Islam. According to Yazidi belief, God created the universe from fragments of a pearl globe. He painted the earth in the bright colors of a peacock's feathers and sent his chief angel, Tawusi Melek, as a link between Himself and the people. On earth, Tawusi Melek took the form of a peacock. When some Iraqis heard about the Peacock Angel, they misinterpreted the imagery and called the Yazidis "devil worshippers." This led to extreme violence directed against the Yazidis, from the time of the Ottoman Empire (1299–1922) to the rise of ISIS (also known as ISIL or Daesh).

Shireen and forty-seven members of her family were caught in the net of ISIS terror that began in August 2014. Eighteen are still missing. She speaks Kurmanji, a Kurdish dialect. Hadi Pir, the vice president of the Yazda Cultural Center in Lincoln, Nebraska, acted as our interpreter. Later, Saad Babir and Laila Khoudeida graciously translated our recordings and correspondence. Laila also provided additional material.

Though reliving the details of her life in captivity is extremely painful, Shireen continues to courageously speak out so that the massacre of her people will not be lost in history's dustbin. Shireen says, "We Yazidis are a simple and peaceful people. We don't hurt anyone. Throughout our history, we have faced persecutions. For this reason, I ask the international community, especially the United States, to protect us. Continue to liberate our abducted people from ISIS captivity. Don't forget us."

Shireen continues, "Anytime I meet someone who escaped from ISIS, I ask them about my family members. Are they still with ISIS? Are they dead? No one has seen them. I keep these pictures with me always because I miss them."

My name is Shireen. I am twenty-six years old. I was born in Rambossy, a village south of Sinjar, in Northern Iraq. I lived on a farm with thirteen members of my family. I am the third child in my family. When I was ten years old, not quite ten years old, my father died of a cardiovascular disease and my mother died from a cerebral vascular sickness. My older sister was married with kids and living away from home. I was the next oldest female at home. I stopped going to school to take care of my younger brothers and sisters. My uncles, aunts, and cousins all lived nearby. We worked in the fields together, growing tomatoes, cucumbers, eggplants, onions, barley, and wheat. Our life was good. We were satisfied with what we had.

On August 3, 2014, ISIS attacked the Yazidi land in the Sinjar district. We were on our farm near Rambossy. My uncle was away, fighting ISIS militants on the border of the Gerzarek village. He called and said, "We are leaving the town because we cannot hold it anymore. You need to go to Sinjar Mountain."

Throughout the Yazidis' history, Mount Sinjar has been their shelter. ISIS already controlled much of the surrounding area.

I prepared food and other necessities to take with us. I baked bread and placed it in a bag. Then I locked our front door from the inside and jumped over the wall. At this point, we didn't know what ISIS would do to us, but I heard rumors that they were taking girls and women to be sold as sex slaves. I asked my brother Ali to kill me and my sisters before anyone could ever touch us. Ali thought I was crazy and told me to stop saying such things. We got in our little pickup truck and headed toward Sinjar Mountain. By the time we arrived at the foothills of the mountain, our car broke down. Ali told the rest of us to start walking up the mountain and that he and his family would follow us later.

My two youngest brothers, Qahtan and Adnam, tried to take our sheep to the mountain. ISIS appeared and shot some rounds to scare them. The militants said, "Don't go anywhere. We're not going to hurt you." My brothers hid among the sheep and then ran away. ISIS captured them, but that was later.

Shireen before captivity

A lot of our men were with us, but they did not have guns. It wouldn't have been so easy to capture us if the men had arms. Some of the men had guns, but they spent all their ammunition earlier, fighting in the town. I was captured with my brothers Dakhil, Hadi, Hadi's son Delhat, and three of my sisters — Nerges and her four children, Khefshe, and Sahera. We were terrified. I called my brother Ali on my cell. He said he couldn't make it to the mountain any faster. We thought that Ali would be captured. He was. Ali, his wife, and his daughter Laila were caught by ISIS at the root of the mountain.

Our family tried to stay in touch with each other. One of my uncles called another uncle on his cell. "Where are you?" While they were speaking, three trucks, each carrying three ISIS men, arrived at the bottom of the mountain. Everything happened quickly. There was chaos as we tried to stay together and seek safety on Mount Sinjar. These men were very dirty. They had black clothes and long hair. Some of them were wearing a sort of sandal. One of the militants had only one eye and a long beard.

They demanded our cell phones, our jewelry, and our weapons. They said they would torture anyone who refused to give them their stuff. I turned off my cell phone and put it in my sock. My sister also turned off her phone and placed it in between her clothes.

The militants ordered the men to take out their personal identification cards from their wallets. My cousin had two phones; he broke one because he did not want ISIS to have access to our phone numbers and the names of our family.

They forced us into their vehicles and drove to a wedding hall in Sinjar, at the bottom of the mountain. There were so many of us. It was very hot, and people suffered from thirst and hunger. Later I heard that a lot of kids died on the mountain because of dehydration and lack of milk and food.

Men and women were separated. Boys older than twelve years were put with the men. I was with my sisters and other family members. My uncle told them, "My family doesn't speak Arabic. I want them with me." One of the ISIS militants put his gun to my uncle's head and said, "I will kill you if you speak any more words." Another man cried, "I want my family." They ordered him to kneel, and they shot him from the back and threw him over a cliff. They did this right in front of us, right in front of his mom and his family.

We started crying, and they told us, "If you cry, we will kill you. Anyone who cries or screams, we will kill you."

My uncle whispered, "Just calm down." There were hundreds of ISIS members threatening to kill anyone who had phones with them. The ISIS fighter, who killed the man, gave his gun to another fighter, who had long hair and was barefoot. The militant was about to kill all the men, but his phone rang. After the call, he said that he was not going to kill any more at this moment.

We were all in a government office inside the city of Sinjar. All the men were put in rooms, and the women stayed in the corridor. At night, they came to take women. My sister Sahera was fifteen years old. She hid behind me and started to vomit because she was so frightened. They took her anyway. I held tight to her hand and begged them not to take her. One of the ISIS militants hit me on my shoulder with the back of his gun and took her. She was a child. I raised her when our parents died, and it was so hard to let her go. She was wearing a dress I had made for her. I thought I must die because I could not bear losing my sister.

A master is prohibited from having intercourse with his female slave who is married to someone else; instead, the master receives her service, [while] the husband [gets to] enjoy her [sexually].

—ISIS pamphlet on the treatment of female slaves

When they started taking all the single women, I put my three-year-old nephew, Delhat, on my bosom. "I'm married, and this is my son!" They left me. But then they came again to take me. I begged them to leave me, and they did. They tried to take my brother's wife, who has a baby. She was crying, "I'm married! I'm married!"

MOSUL

After some days, ISIS took all us women to Mosul. I begged them to take me to my sister Sahera. They just laughed at me.

ISIS used a government facility to distribute the Yazidi women to their fighters. ISIS men came and bought women and girls. We were given black clothes, long dresses, and head covers [hijabs]. I was able to stay with my family because I claimed I was married to my cousin, Khairy, and that my nephew Delhat, my brother Hadi's child, was my son. [ISIS had separated Hadi's wife from the rest of the family.]

The next day, the ISIS militants walked us back to the PDK [Barzani Party] headquarters. They put the Kurdistan and PKK flags on the ground and made everybody step on them. *[The Kurdistan Workers' Party, or PKK (Partiya Karkerên Kurdistanê in Kurdish), is a leftist organization based in Turkey and Iraq.]*

Airplanes overhead were bombing all around the building, and glass from the windows started to fly at us. The bombs were too close. Pieces of glass injured two sides of my nephew's head. We all tried to run through a small door. Once we were outside, we didn't see any ISIS fighters. It was a chance to escape, but after a moment, they came at us from all sides and we were abducted again.

They put us in trucks and moved us to an area close to the Mosul city called Badoosh. There was a huge prison there that had been run by the Iraqi government before ISIS came. It smelled terrible. Much of Badoosh was burned and we saw blood on the ground. We thought that ISIS killed people there.

My nephew was still with me. We stayed in the Badoosh prison for about seven days. We were given food once a day, one *samon* [Iraqi bread roll] for each person, and one piece of cheese. Because we were so frightened and scared, and worried about the kids, we didn't eat that food at all. We gave it to the kids.

There was no drinking water for two days. Kids were crying for water. I think some of the kids died of thirst.

My uncle's wife, Junay, my brother Ali's wife, Layla, and my sister Khefshe were with me. We didn't know about anyone else in the family. My sister and I scratched ashes from the wall and put them on our faces so that we wouldn't look pretty and would not be selected by ISIS fighters.

The ISIS fighters brought us the dirty water that they used to wash their bodies. They made us abducted people drink that dirty body water. Because of the thirst, some people were obligated to drink. I could not drink. They brought us rotten grapes to eat. The smell all around us grew worse because there were no restrooms; there were feces everywhere.

In the morning, they brought a girl that was covered all in black clothes. She could barely walk. I ran toward her and asked her about Sahera. She said she had not heard Sahera's name. The girl was telling us that the ISIS militants raped her and that they had been raping all the girls, especially those who resisted reading the Quran.

Then the ISIS fighters took all the kids and put them in a pen outside. They laughed and told us that they were going to kill the kids. Women and girls started crying and screaming. "We're not going to kill them." The ISIS fighters laughed at us more. They said that it was time to give the kids an Islamic education, teachings from Islamic religious texts from the Quran. We stayed in that terrible prison for about a week.

When an airplane flew overhead, the abductors brought the kids back inside the building. The next day, the ISIS headquarters that was close to where we were staying was hit by a bomb. Bombs fell all around us. The militants got buses to move us to another place. As we were taken outside, airplanes appeared to drop more bombs. All the ISIS militants disappeared again. They just left us there, out in the open. We couldn't tell who was bombing the area, the Iraqi forces or the U.S. We wanted to hide, but where could we go? Once the airplanes left, the militants came back and started loading us into buses. They moved us to a city close to Sinjar called Tal Afar.

Just before we reached Tal Afar, the ISIS militants separated all the old women from the younger ones. If a woman had gray hair, they took her away. We thought that they killed them all, but once we reached Tal Afar, they were all there.

In Tal Afar, there was another building, like a jail, where they put us. Five ISIS fighters were at the door to the prison. They asked again if we had cell phones, money, and jewelry. They said that they would punish and harm anyone who didn't give them those things. I hid my cell phone in my nephew's diaper. As each woman went inside, they put a light on her face because it was nighttime. They picked women who were pretty and young. One of them wanted to take me, but his colleague said, "Leave this one. She's married."

An ISIS militant said to me, "Are you married?"

I replied, "Yes."

"Is your husband among the men that we abducted?"

"Yes."

Because I claimed I married my cousin and he was among the abducted men, they left me alone.

They took a lot of women that night. They took anyone unmarried, including my sister Khefshe. I was crying. I wanted to beg them to bring my sister back, but my uncle's wife said, "Calm down, or they will take you too. They will separate you from us."

The women and girls taken by the ISIS fighters were sold and used as sex slaves. I've seen women sold for as little as one dollar. I later became one of the women. I was sold five times.

12
For Sale

After seven days, ISIS was getting ready to move us again. We were told that if we converted to Islam, they would bring back our men, and we could live free. They asked me again if I was married.

"Yes, I'm married."

"Who are you married to?"

"I married my cousin." They asked me to swear in God's name that I married my cousin. I swore.

At this point, Layla, my uncle's wife, stood up to them. "We don't want to move to another town. We don't believe you will take us to our men." To persuade us, the ISIS militants took out a phone and called the place where my uncle was being held. They gave him a phone. My uncle told his wife that it's okay to convert to Islam under threat and pressure, because they killed many people who refused to convert.

He said, "Do whatever they ask you to do. Say you will convert to Islam to protect yourself. In the bottom of our hearts, we know that God will forgive us because He knows what's going on. You will remain Yazidi in your soul."

We still didn't believe our abductors. The militants brought my brother Dakhil to us to prove that they did not kill the men. Dakhil was in a jail in the same town that we were in. It had been twelve days since I saw my brother. I didn't believe that he was alive. When I saw him, I fainted. I did not recognize him.

Dakhil told us, "If we do not convert, they will kill us all." Then they brought all the men to us. Our men were so dirty. Their hair was dirty. Their beards had become long.

During this whole time, we could hear bombs falling from the airplanes. They ordered everyone outside to a trench wall, where we hid. There were hundreds of us hiding behind a wall made of soil. Giant ants started eating off the babies and young children. Once the airplanes left, they put all of us, men and women, in buses and took us to two tiny villages called Kaser al-Muhrad and Qizlel Qelo. They put us in a house that had five dead cows, dead chickens, and many dirty things. The smell was filthy, and we had a hard time breathing. I believe that these two villages were once Shiite towns; all the people had run away or were killed.

All our men had been taken there and used as slave laborers to build mosques. The reason why they were building the mosques was because they were converting us to Islam, and they needed a place to teach Islam and the Quran. We stayed here for three months.

I still insisted that I was married to my cousin Khairy. He stayed with me at night, but they would take him away every day to work and receive Islamic teaching.

From mid-August to mid-December, Shireen held tight to her phone. The phone, along with a wedding band her grandmother had once given her, were her lifelines.

ISIS militants were constantly checking us for cell phones because they knew that some people were contacting the outside. When my cousin went to the mosque, I left my nephew with his mother and hid in a hole. It was a big hole that was a good hiding spot. I hid because I was afraid that they would search me, and I still had my phone. Remember I had turned it off and hid it in my shoe. We did not have chargers and there was little battery life left, but still, I would not let go of my phone.

One day, one of the men tried to escape. ISIS militants shot and killed him and brought his dead body back to us. "If anyone tries to escape, we will do the same thing we did to this man." My uncle said that nobody should try to escape, because we had a lot of kids with us. "These people have no mercy," my uncle told us. There was no escape.

One night, my uncle's daughter, Parween, was taken away by an ISIS militant. She was forced to marry this militant under Sharia law [the term for law based on the Quran]. A few days later, the militant brought her back to visit us. The ISIS militant wrote a note to my uncle that said, "We just bring your daughter for a visit, and we give you this note to let you know that we know she is with you. If she escapes and tries to run away, we will punish you. We will kill you."

Another night, I was with my uncle when they came to search his house. His wife was somewhere else. They asked my uncle, "Who is this one?"

My uncle said, "No, no, this is my wife." Because they didn't know my uncle's wife, they believed him for some reason. They left.

During the Roji and Eda Rojiet Ezi holiday, we secretly fasted for three days. The militants forced the men to drink water and say the Muslim prayers. They tried to make us eat rotten food. I did not have the appetite to eat anything.

MOSUL

After our fasting holiday, they crammed us into buses with no windows. It was very dark. People were standing on top of one another and walking on each other. It was hard to breathe, and people were vomiting. At night, we arrived in Mosul. There were three-story buildings in Mosul, and they gave a room to each family. I still claimed that my nephew Delhat was my son, so they left him with me. They gave another room to my brother Hadi, Delhat's real father. Hadi had claimed that our sister Nerges was his wife. Sometimes Delhat, who was only three years old, would cry for his parents, but I managed to keep him quiet when ISIS members came around.

Once we were in this building, the militants brought ISIS women to search our bodies, our hair, our clothes, and everywhere. They were again looking for cell phones, jewelry, and money. The focus was cell phones. They found some religious stuff on some of the Yazidi women. When we Yazidis go to our holy place, the Lalish Temple, we take some of the earth to keep with us — all Yazidi families have soil from Lalish Temple — so they found some of those things on the old Yazidi women and men. They took the women and a couple of the men away. We thought they would kill them, and I think probably they did. They searched us again, even our bodies, looking for anything that belonged to the Yazidi religion.

I asked my cousin Khairy to write my name on my arm in English letters with a needle, like a tattoo. If I was able to commit suicide, I wanted my family to know it was me. I told my brothers and my uncles that if the militants came back to take me, I was going to kill myself. I would not allow them to rape me and bring me back to visit my family like they did the other girls. My uncle told me that if they took me, it was against my will, so it didn't count as a sin. My brothers told me that if I tried to kill myself, they would never forgive me.

Then the ISIS militants brought a Quran and asked all the families to swear on it that we are a family. For example, they asked my uncle if these two women — me and his real wife — are his wives. My uncle swore that we were his wives. Another group asked my cousin to swear that I was his wife. He swore. Everybody was swearing.

Shireen shows her tattoo, which uses an alternate spelling of her name.

One of my cousins spoke Arabic. He went to the militants and said, "Okay, we've done everything you've asked us to do. What else do you want? Yes, we swear, these people are our family." But the ISIS militants did not believe him, and they took the men away to a different place.

The next morning, I had a terrible headache because I had not slept the night before. Delhat was on my lap when the militants came rushing into our room. They took Delhat from me and forced me and Khairy down stairs along with others who pretended that they were married. About fourteen of us were pretending to be couples. They separated the men from the women and brought the Quran for us to swear that the Yazidi men were truly our husbands. Khairy begged them and cried. He told the militants that I was his wife and that they should leave us alone. The militants laughed and said that we could not fool them with our tricks.

We were taken in buses again. I was sure that they were going to separate us from our family. I kissed the barrel of ISIS pistols, begging them not to take us. But they did not listen.

Again, they asked the men to swear that we were their family, their wives. They put a man in a blanket and started shooting at the blanket. They wanted us to think that they had killed that man so that we would be frightened. Later I learned that they had not killed him.

I worried that ISIS would kill my cousin Khairy. I felt guilty because it would be my fault if they killed him. He lied about us being a married couple to save me, and now he himself was in danger.

ISIS militants loaded all the women into a bus and took us to a courthouse. I could see my brothers crying as they took us away. My youngest brother was shouting to me not to do anything to myself. I never saw Khairy again. He is among the missing.

We met another Yazidi woman at the courthouse. She had already been married to an ISIS militant, but he had been killed. She said, "I know what they will do to you, because this is my second time here. They will sell you."

After they locked us in a room, we tried to kill ourselves by pulling our scarves around our necks. Another woman stopped us. She said, "Killing is not a solution. After you kill yourself, they will throw your bodies to the animals. You will still be humiliated. Dying won't help you here."

A girl who knew Arabic asked the ISIS militant what they will do to us. One of them replied, "We are waiting for Abu Ali, Haji Mehdi, and the judge to decide." Abu Ali is one of the ISIS militants that was a prince of ISIS. He was older and had a long beard. He dressed in black. Haji Mehdi was also an ISIS militant. He was younger, thin, had a beard, and long hair. The judge was a prince of ISIS too, but I do not know anything about him.

They arrived with a camera and took our pictures. Haji Mehdi asked us questions: "How old are you? Where are you from?" They asked about our fathers and mothers. We were all careful not to answer that we were from a town that resisted ISIS, because we expected that they would kill us. Everybody said they were from Sinjar City. I did too.

That night, they brought us bread and eggs. I did not eat anything.

The next day, they separated us again. They brought in a lady, a Muslim doctor. She told Haji Mehdi that she could tell who is married and who is single just by looking at us. I recognized her voice. I knew her! She was a doctor in Sinjar. Many times, before ISIS came, we visited her clinic. Her name is Nawal. NAWAL!

Nawal said that we were lying, that only two of us were married and the rest were virgins. The judge selected four girls and gave each of them to an ISIS fighter.

All this time, I was wearing a long robe called a *dishdasha* in Arabic. The girl who spoke Arabic got black clothes for us. She told us to put on the clothes and be ready. Haji Mehdi, Abu Ali, and the judge were going to distribute us to ISIS fighters and other people who lived in the Islamic State. I washed my hands, but I didn't wash my face. I became confused, dizzy, because I hadn't had food for three days. I was so frightened, I passed out.

When I became conscious, I could not walk. I thought, this is my opportunity to get away from them. I pretended that I could not talk. The only sound I made was to cry.

My friends put a blanket on me. The girl who spoke Arabic called to the guard, "Why do you punish us? Even when someone gets sick, you don't want to help them. She passed out and cannot move and cannot talk. She needs to go to a doctor."

"We don't have permission to call a doctor," the fighter said. "We must wait for Abu Ali and Haji Mehdi to come back." After a while, they sent Nawal, the doctor who said that we were virgins, to the hospital with me.

In the hospital, they wanted to prove that I was lying, so they stuck needles in my feet to see if I would move. I kept silent, with no movement. No talking. No talking at all. Then the doctor told the militants that I probably had a stroke. They gave me an IV infusion, some syrup, and pills. Then they took me back to the prison. They told the girl who spoke Arabic to give me the medications.

The girls told me to eat and drink and that they would not tell anyone, but I did not trust anyone at this point, so I remained pretending to be paralyzed.

In the morning, the militants came in and told us that an imam, a religious man, was coming. All the girls started crying.

The imam entered and asked if I had talked or eaten. He brought a bag filled with black burkas for us to wear. We were told to go shower and dress in the black clothes. Afterwards, one girl, Berevan, was sold off to one of the militants who was already married. Then they sold Alia. She hugged all of us before she left. She was crying and said that this was the end of all of us. Then they sold my friend Maha, who later managed to escape and is now in Germany. They then took another girl. That day they sold off four of the girls. The next day, the militants came for a fifth girl. The other girls used to joke with her because she was very skinny. They'd tell her that she is lucky because they would not want to take her. She was taken away to be seen by a militant, but he did not want to marry her, so she came back.

Then they came for me.

13
The Black Hole
of Captivity

Three of the militants covered me in black fabric, picked me up, and took me to the room where the holy man was selling us. The holy man uncovered my face and said that I looked okay. Haji Mehdi had supposedly taken me for himself, but because I did not talk or walk, he sold me to an elderly militant, Abu Anas from Baaj.

Abu means "father" in Arabic. Abu Anas is not his real name. Shireen says that none of the ISIS militants used real names.

Abu Anas was from one of the Arabic tribes who live in Baaj, west of Mosul. He bought me and took me to his house. He was already married and had a big family.

His wife met me with five of their children. She kissed me and said I should eat some food. I still did not walk or talk. Abu Anas was rich, so he took me to a separate house from his wife and children. There were a lot of Yazidi girls there.

That night he came to the room. I was terrified. He removed the blanket that covered me. I insisted on not moving. Abu Anas said I was lying, and he bit my feet to test me. "Tomorrow I will marry you," he said. He tried to rape me, but I pretended that I was sick. I did not move at all.

The next night, he came in the room again and told me he was going to marry me. I started crying but did not make a move. He brought two other militants into the room. This was the most difficult time for me because I was terrified at the thought that they were going to gang-rape me. But instead, they brought the Quran to my face and laughed and made fun of me and my religion. One of them prayed over some water and placed his hand on my head, saying a prayer that I talk.

Abu Anas told me that even if I did not talk or walk, he was still going to marry me. Then all three fell asleep. I did not sleep that night at all. I stared at them the whole night. When they woke up, they ate breakfast. The two other militants left, and Abu Anas started to molest me. He grabbed my hands and stepped on my feet. It was so painful. I still did not move, so he left.

For three days, Abu Anas tried to rape me. I resisted by pretending I was sick and unconscious. Finally, he decided to get rid of me. He sold me to Abu Ali for one hundred dollars.

Abu Ali took me back to Mosul, back to the jail where the girls were originally waiting to be sold. Only two girls were left, the skinny one and another who had a head injury and was not mentally stable. The second girl was very pretty and spoke Arabic well. Apparently I fainted again, because when I woke up, I found myself in a hospital in Mosul. The pretty girl was with me.

Because Abu Ali had bought me, he stayed in the hospital. After four days, they inserted a urine tube inside me. That was very painful. Abu Ali threatened to have me gang-raped if I didn't move. I prayed to God that I would die before Abu Ali touched me.

Abu Ali took me back to the prison and put me in a room with a pretty Christian woman. He said, "This Christian woman is crazy." She had suffered so much she had lost her mind. I wouldn't talk with her because she might be an informer. They brought us food that I refused to eat. I gave my food to the Christian woman. After she ate some, she screamed and shouted with a high, high voice while putting the rest of the food in her hair. Sometimes she would come sit by me and hold my hand and cry. Then she would take off all of her clothes and start screaming. She frightened me when she did this. I stayed in that jail for about a week.

Abu Ali sold me to another militant for one dollar. His name was Abu Adel. Abu Adel had a long blond beard and curly hair. He said that he was a doctor living in Syria and that he would fix me himself. Three militants came and dragged me with a blanket to his car. He stopped in front of another prison that kept Yazidi girls and women and picked up two more girls. He told them to speak to me in our language so that I would respond. I did not speak.

When we reached Syria, I was very nauseous and passed out again. Abu Adel drove me to a hospital. They said that I had an infection from the bladder bag they had inserted into me. Two nurses dressed in burkas made fun of me because I smelled bad. They gave me an IV and I was released.

Abu Adel drove us to a place where they sold Yazidi girls. I saw a girl sold to a man who spoke a Kurdish language. He said that he loved his wife, but she only gave him one child. He wanted more children. Then the Kurdish man pointed to me. Abu Adel said, "This one is mine. I bought her in Iraq."

The two militants and the two Yazidi girls spent the night together. In the morning, we were given tea and yogurt for breakfast. I did not eat.

Abu Adel was mean. He brought some other people to the house who had something green in color, like oily medicine. They said that this stuff would make me

157

talk. They forced the Yazidi women to restrain me. They cried as they grabbed my hands and my legs. Horrible green oily liquid was poured in my mouth. I tried not to swallow it. I fought back as much as I could. I knew I was about to die. Despite what they did, I didn't speak. Now, sometimes, I still feel that liquid in my mouth. It's hard to eat oily foods. When I think about that time, I feel the taste in my mouth. I feel that taste now, just thinking about it. I taste it.

After that, they brought in an imam. He read the Quran to me. He brought some water and tried to make me drink this water. I didn't take it. I made no movement. No talk. He threw the water in my face.

Abu Adel and one of the other militants were cousins. They were originally from Turkey, and the cousin's mother was angry at him for joining ISIS. His plan was to marry a Yazidi woman, buy a lot of gold, and return to Turkey. The cousin asked Abu Adel why I didn't talk. "I will make her talk," he said.

The militants dressed me in a burka and took me to a hospital. They removed my head scarf and started laughing. Three workers put me in a wheelchair and pushed me inside. Abu Adel was already there, dressed in a white gown because he was a doctor. He gave me an IV and medicine.

Up to this point they called me Hamdya, because they didn't know my real name. But once my arm was exposed, they saw the tattoo that my fake-husband-real-cousin had scratched on my arm. Abu Adel asked the other Yazidi woman, "Why does she have a tattoo? Is it religious or something? If it's religious, I'm going to have it taken off." They kept on calling me Hamdya because that was an Arabic name and Shireen was a Yazidi name.

The cousin took the Yazidi girl away and I was alone. After a while, Abu Adel returned and said that I looked better. He played Quran verses on his phone that was placed by my head.

That night, they brought in another Yazidi girl to try to get me to speak. She was from Kocho and her name was Noura. She had been sold into marriage to an

ISIS doctor who treated wounded ISIS fighters. This doctor was a specialist who had examined my reflex to pain earlier by putting a needle in my foot. Noura told me to cooperate with them or else I would be harmed. When I did not speak, she returned to the others after promising me that she would see me again. By now I was very weak and dizzy. I was having delusions and could not feel anything. I watched the door to myself lock.

The next morning, Abu Adel left cake in my room to see if I would eat it. When I did not, he became very angry with me. He told me to get ready because he was going to marry me and take me.

A third doctor, a woman, came into the room. She was very scary. She wore sunglasses, had many weapons around her body, and spoke loudly in English. After she examined me, she said that I was suffering from panic attack, that there was no benefit trying to make me talk, and that we needed to go to another hospital. Whenever doctors said that I had a heart attack or a panic attack, it made me happy because I was looking for any chance to get rid of them.

At the new hospital, they put me in a big machine, like a CT scan or an MRI. When I saw that machine, I was so afraid. The report from the test was that there was nothing wrong with me and that I was lying. The head doctor did not speak Arabic, only English. Later, this English-speaking doctor checked my vital signs and said that I had had a stroke. Again, that made me happy.

The next morning, Abu Adel was so angry with me that he stood on my feet. The English-speaking doctor came as well and checked my joints to see if I could move my body. When I did not move, he pushed me off the bed and I fell to the ground. Two nurses picked me up and put me back on the bed.

The English-speaking woman doctor with weapons around her body and another doctor arrived with a bunch of wires that they placed all over my body — on my ears, my toes, feet, stomach, and back. I thought it was to test my heart, or maybe my virginity. I was wrong. It was to give me electric-shock treatment. They told me that this technique is used for people who suffered from schizophrenia or other mental problems. They said that they used this on people who did not respond to medications. They practically electrocuted me.

While this was happening, the doctors and nurses above me were laughing. I remembered a time when my family and I were in our home in Sinjar. I remembered watching a Turkish show on TV where they electrocuted a guy. We were crying for this guy. I never, ever, thought something this terrible could happen to me. But it was happening to me. Even today, when I walk, I feel pain in my leg and foot from the electricity.

After they shocked me, I was totally numb. I didn't know what was going on around me. I couldn't open my eyes. After seven days with only an IV, I could open my eyes, but I couldn't move. The two Yazidi girls came to my room and begged me to talk. They swore by the Quran that if I talked, I would be taken to my family. I knew that they were forced to say this. I did not talk.

Three other ISIS fighters came, and I was very afraid because I knew that they were going to torture me again. They covered me with the blanket and pulled me out into the garden. They put another blanket on my face and my head. Abu Adel said, "Now we are going to make her speak." They pointed a pistol at my head and said that they will kill me if I don't speak. The two Yazidi women were there, screaming and begging them not to kill me. While laughing, they fired two shots close my head. Even now I feel the sound of two shots in my ear. At that point, I did not care anymore. I preferred to die. Death was better than this miserable situation, so I was not afraid. Kill me or not kill me, I didn't talk.

They carried me back to my room and put me on the bed. One of them was laughing at me so hard he fell on the ground. I think they didn't kill me because we women are a good business for ISIS.

Abu Adel took me back to the same prison in Mosul where the Christian lady was being held. She was still there, eating a little rice and pouring the rest on her head. The Christian lady had urinated all over the cell, and the smell was so awful I could not breathe. Also, my blanket was filthy because I had been covering myself under it for months, even when I had my period. I could not wash the blanket.

Abu Adel sold me to another doctor, Abu Omar, for two dollars. The next day, Abu Omar took me to a nearby hospital, where I was given an IV line and some IV fluids. The liquid solutions are what probably kept me from starving to death. I stayed in the hospital for two days before I was taken to Abu Omer's house, which was about fourteen minutes from the hospital.

Abu Omer had three daughters and one son. The youngest daughter, Aysha, would pull my hair. His son-in-law had been hit during an airplane raid and was on crutches. The son-in-law asked if I had relatives in Kurdistan. He promised to call them if I gave him their numbers. He even said that if I talked, he would take me to Kurdistan. I did not give him my relatives' numbers. I only stared at him, and sometimes tears would fall from my eyes. I could control my movement, but I could not control my tears.

In Abu Omar's house, I slept on the floor in a locked room. It was so cold, my teeth chattered. Because I didn't want them to hear the noise, I forced myself to stop shivering. At this point, I had not eaten real food in months and could barely open my eyes.

After three days, Abu Omar, his wife, and his daughter took me back to the hospital. I was put into a room and they locked the door. Not one person took pity on me. Abu Omer claimed that he would be nice to me if I spoke. I didn't respond to him. I heard some doctors say that they were going to operate on me. I reached out with my hands, begging them not to do this. The doctors, who were speaking in English, took me to the operating room and put two IV lines in me. Abu Omar's wife tried to take from my finger the ring my grandmother had given me, but I resisted her. With my hand, I told her NO, NO. That ring was the only proof I had that I was married. Another doctor, a man with a long beard, came. He was ISIS too. I think he was an anesthesiologist, because he had two syringes of medication. As soon as he pushed a drug through an IV line, I went to sleep.

When I woke up from the anesthesia, I saw Abu Omar's wife asleep beside me. I was restrained to the wall. There was a bandage on my stomach area and I was in so much pain. I threw up on my hospital gown and was very dizzy. Then I passed out. (To this day, I don't know why they did that. They did not take my organs.) Another lady was in the bed next to mine, but she had passed away. When I saw her dead body, I passed out again. The next time I woke up, Abu Omar and two nurses were looking down at me. Two IV bags were connected to me, one was filled with urine and the other was filled with blood.

Abu Omar's wife gave me back my grandmother's ring, and they took me to their house. They carried me to the third floor of their big house. My stitches opened, and I felt excruciating pain in my back and stomach. I thought I was about to die.

One day, a very tall man armed with weapons came to the house. The first thing he did was step on my legs. Then they put me in a wheelchair and took me back down to the ground floor. A black truck, with windows covered with black glass, arrived at Abu Omar's house. They put me in the truck and covered me with a blanket. I was suffering severe pain due to the surgery.

By now I understood them, these ISIS drivers, when they talked on their walkie-talkies. I heard them say that they had to change their directions because there were land mines on the main road that could blow us up. We arrived back in Tal Afar. Haji Mehdi, Abu Ali, and the judge were no longer there. A new judge was in charge. He decided to release me. He wrote my name on a piece of paper and signed it.

The drivers took me to a place with many buses. About two hundred Yazidis were there. (I recognized them by their clothes.) All of them were old or disabled or had diseases. They—we—were no longer a benefit for ISIS. They couldn't sell us as sex slaves.

Shireen just after her release

The buses took us to Hawija, which is near Kirkuk city. There, Kurdish Peshmerga forces received us and brought us to Erbil city. From Erbil, they took us to Lalish, our holiest temple. My brothers Kurdo and Qahtan came running toward the bus. They were crying as they helped me out of the bus and onto a wheelchair. Even then I did not speak, because I was not sure that we were rid of ISIS. When we reached the temple, I kissed the hand of our spiritual leader, Baba Sheikh, as an act of respect, and I spoke. "Please try to do something for other Yazidis who are still in ISIS captivity."

14
After

After I was released, I hoped that my family was saved too. My sisters Sahera and Khefshe had already escaped, and we were reunited.

Sahera had been sent to Rabia, a city one mile from the Syrian border, where Arabs from the Shammar tribe live. Another Yazidi girl, who was abducted with my sister, was with her. They had decided to escape captivity. They took some clothes and ran from the house to another house. They were not sure if the family in one of the houses would help them. But one did. In the house, a man contacted our family and asked if they would pay him for Sahera's release. My family did not have money with them, but my brother Qahtan took out loans from friends and neighbors who had brought money with them. Sahera and the other girl were taken to Syria — that's where the Kurds were, the PKK [the Kurdistan Workers' Party]. The PKK transferred them safely to our family.

Khefshe told me that she and another Yazidi girl were put in a house they knew well because it had once belonged to an Iraqi parliament member. They were treated very badly. They were beaten and forced to cook and clean for their captors. When they were about to be moved, the other abducted girl ran away. My sister remained in captivity.

Khefshe said that she was so frightened when her friend escaped. When the ISIS militants asked about the other girl, she told them, "I don't know where she went." It was nighttime, and the ISIS militants started to look for her. While they were busy looking, Khefshe ran from the house. She hid between buildings and rocks, anything to keep away from ISIS eyes. She told me that the ISIS fighters had flashlights and were close to where she was hiding. She was afraid a dog would bark at her and reveal her hiding place. When they looked someplace else, she ran, taking the same road where we were when we were captured. This time she made it. She reached Yazidi fighters and was saved.

My three-year-old nephew Delhat stayed in captivity for three years. He was finally ransomed through PKK. The PKK returned some ISIS members for Delhat, along with six other members of my family, including my sister Nerges and her four kids.

I moved to a refugee camp called Bajed Kandala. A member of the Yazda Center in Nebraska visited the camp to give psychological support to us survivors. I helped cook for the Yazda employees who were helping us. After about a year, the Yazda Center arranged a visa for me to come to America.

In July 2017, Mosul was liberated. We were so happy because we expected the remaining captured Yazidis would come back. But there are very few in number. Thousands of Yazidis had been killed. Thousands of them were kidnapped. Hundreds of thousands are displaced. Dozens of mass graves are everywhere. I personally know a woman from Kocho village whose three kids were poisoned by ISIS. While all this was happening, no one tried to help us. No one did anything to stop them. No one is ready to protect our mass graves.

I would like to live in my homeland, but I can't. The people who lived beside us as neighbors became ISIS. They were the first to attack us, to hurt us. And now they are living safely in Kurdistan, under KRG [Kurdistan regional government] protection. No one talks of them or gives an account of what they did to us. Nobody wants to go to court to ask why they did this to us. Many Muslim people around Sinjar joined ISIS and committed atrocities against Yazidis. My cousin saw one of his college friends with ISIS. My brother saw his teacher with ISIS. This is the reason why I don't want to go back to Iraq. In Iraq, we lost everything. In Iraq, our family members are still missing. In Iraq, I would see the people who did this to us every day. I would have to deal with them every day. I can't do this.

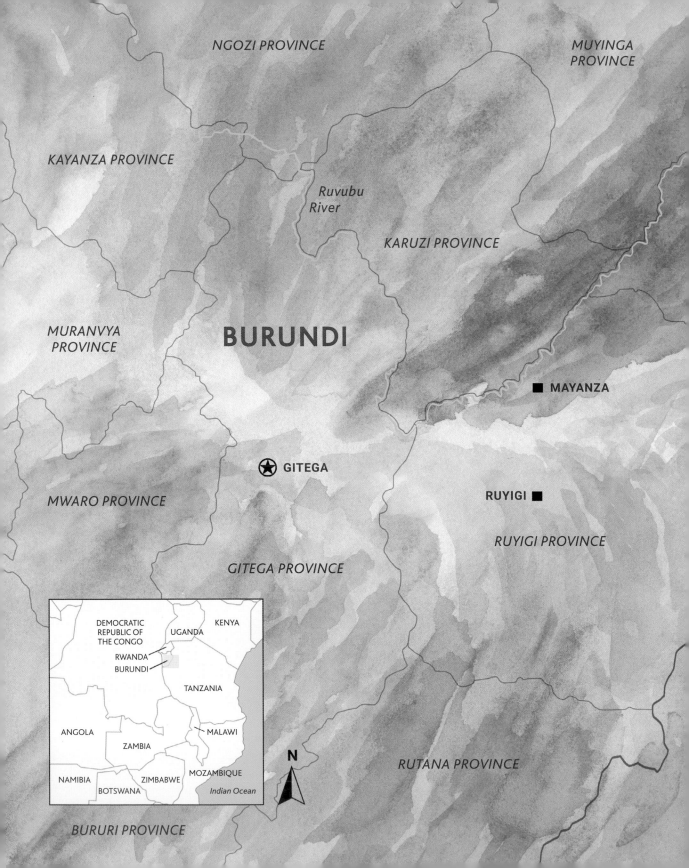

NGOZI PROVINCE

MUYINGA PROVINCE

KAYANZA PROVINCE

Ruvubu River

KARUZI PROVINCE

MURANVYA PROVINCE

BURUNDI

■ MAYANZA

⍟ GITEGA

RUYIGI ■

MWARO PROVINCE

RUYIGI PROVINCE

GITEGA PROVINCE

DEMOCRATIC REPUBLIC OF THE CONGO

KENYA

UGANDA

RWANDA

BURUNDI

TANZANIA

ANGOLA

MALAWI

ZAMBIA

NAMIBIA

ZIMBABWE

MOZAMBIQUE

BOTSWANA

Indian Ocean

N

RUTANA PROVINCE

BURURI PROVINCE

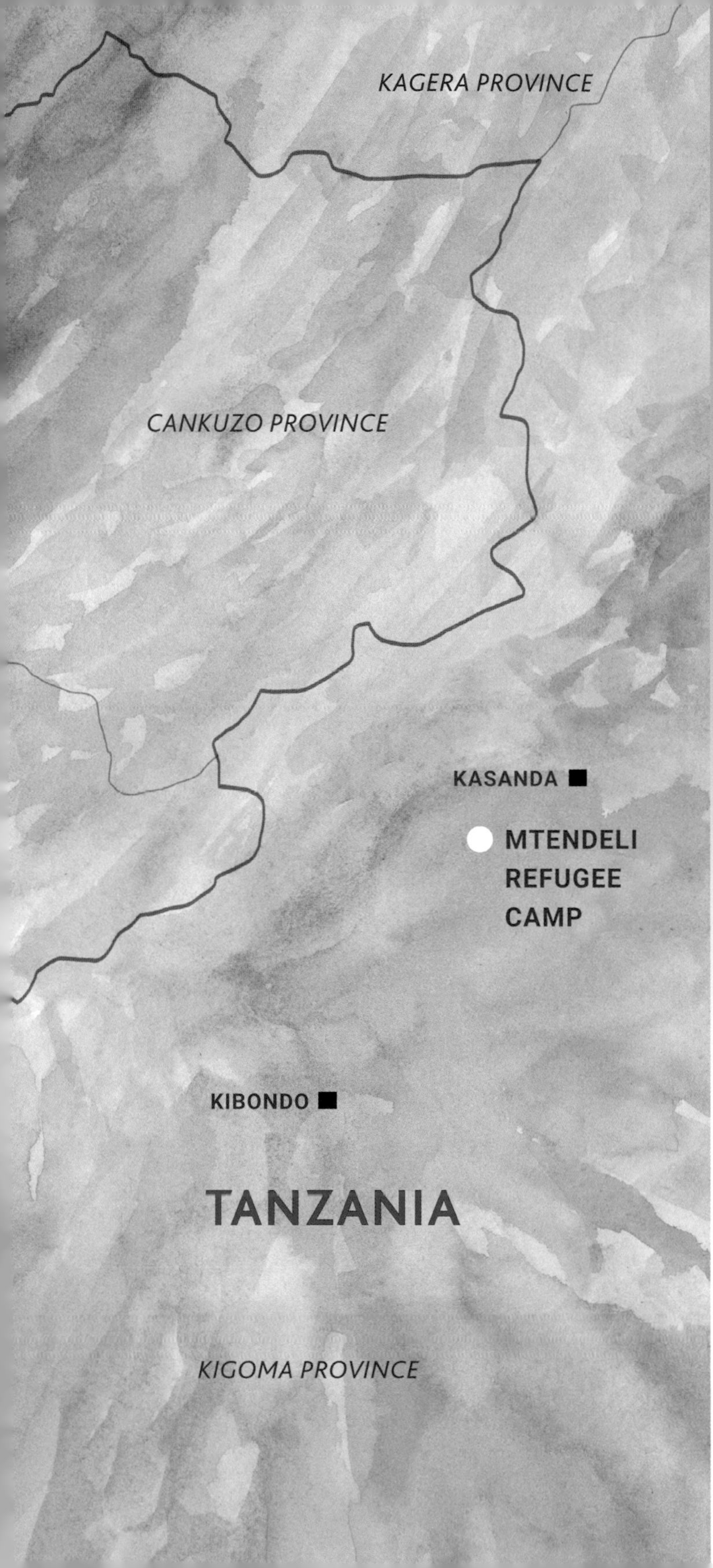

KAGERA PROVINCE

CANKUZO PROVINCE

KASANDA ■

● MTENDELI
REFUGEE
CAMP

KIBONDO ■

TANZANIA

KIGOMA PROVINCE

PART V
HOME

Dieudonné

COUNTRY OF ORIGIN:
Burundi

ETHNIC GROUP:
Hutu and Tutsi

Dieudonné

15
Early One Morning

Much has been reported about the 1994 massacre of Tutsis by Hutus in Rwanda, but few know much about the one in neighboring Burundi, where Hutus went house to house with spears, knives, guns, and machetes, killing Tutsis. Burundi, an impoverished, landlocked country in East-Central Africa, has experienced numerous conflicts between the two ethnic groups, even though the Hutu and Tutsi generally share the same religious beliefs (Christianity), culture, and language (Kirundi, Swahili, and French).

On July 1, 1962, Burundi won its independence from Belgium. Although the majority of the population was Hutu, the Tutsi held most of the power. This led to unending Hutu rebellions and brutal Tutsi retaliations. The cycle of war and peace (mostly war) between the two groups continues.

...

In 1989, Dieudonné was born to a Tutsi mother and a Hutu father. He is the youngest of five children, two boys and three girls. Three siblings — Veronica, Balthazar, and Dieudonné — live in Nebraska; Virginia and Suazis are still in a refugee camp in Africa.

Dieudonné says, "I was four years old when the 1993 genocide of my people began. I remember all of it, every detail of that horrible day when it all began. Every. Single. Detail. It hurt me so much, I can't forget. I will never forget. Maybe it hurt so much just for the purpose to tell this story."

It was early in the morning, and my mom was in the backyard, working in her vegetable garden. We lived by a village called Mayanza, in Ruyigi Province, Burundi, where big-time farmers like my dad grew everything we ever wanted. We had uncountable fruit trees. We had cattle. The only things we bought in the store were clothes. Everything else we grew or raised.

In our culture, the eldest male child inherits the land from the father. My dad was the only son in his family, and all his family's land went to him. Our house was one of the most beautiful homes in the area, with large glass windows and French doors. My dad had recently built it, and we had just moved in.

That morning, we kids were in our bedrooms when we heard a loud banging at the door. We ran to the window to see who was there so early in the morning. Some men who lived in the village were standing at the door covered in blood, holding machetes.

My dad calmly went to the door and greeted the men. "You need to take care of your wife," they said. Those men could have easily rushed into the house and killed my mom, but because my father was Hutu and highly respected, they did not. Instead they said, "You need to kill your wife. Otherwise we will come back and kill your whole family." We kids were at the window, listening, watching the entire thing.

With incredible composure, my dad said, "Yeah, for sure. I'll take care of it." And the men left to hunt for — to kill — more.

My dad closed the door, turned back inside the house, grabbed me — I was the baby, four years old — and ran to the backyard. He pulled my mom out of the garden, and we started running. We did not even look back at the house. In a split second, my dad had decided that the most endangered people were my mom and me, the little one. Because they were older, my father believed that my brother and sisters would be okay. They hid in the house, and we ran, and ran, and ran. Our destination was the border of Tanzania, about thirty-five miles away. My father knew that if we could cross to Tanzania, we'd be safe. We didn't have a car. We lived by a village, in the countryside; we didn't need cars. The trip to the border took longer than usual because we couldn't take a straight route. We zigzagged through the jungle in order to avoid where my dad thought the killers might be.

Throughout the day, we saw many people dead or dying. The rivers that we crossed, rivers that were once crystal-clear water, were now flowing red with blood. We were totally alone, terrified, thinking someone could catch us at any time. It was horrific.

Towards the end of the day, we made it to the border. There's a big, deep river that divides Tanzania and Burundi. People at the river who had carved traditional canoes from the trunks of trees helped us cross. Once we crossed the river, we searched for a hiding spot. Monkeys were everywhere. It seemed as if they were following us. When we stopped at a pond to drink water, the monkeys in the trees threw things at us.

There was one moment I will never forget. We were walking in the bush and came face-to-face with a whole family of gorillas. My dad said that gorillas disrespected women. If they find a woman, they will either beat her or chase her away. They feared men, though. And then my father proved it. With his machete in his hand he called to them — *ngoo, ngoo. Ngoo* means "come." The gorillas didn't come. My father handed the machete to my mom and called again, *ngoo, ngoo.* They started coming closer and closer. They weren't threatened by my mom. My father grabbed the machete and they ran away. That was crazy.

Soon thereafter, my father found a hiding place behind some bushes. There were a few other people hiding there as well. He left us and walked back home to get the rest of my siblings. By the end of the second day, we were all together again.

There was no food, no clean water, no beds, no bathrooms, and we still were not safe. There were rumors that the killers were following people even to the Tanzania side.

After a week or so, some of the people who were hiding with us got sick. We were afraid to come out to seek help. My mom became one of those people. To this day we don't know what made her sick, because there was no doctor to diagnose anything. . . . Give me a minute. . . . That's the moment that hits me the most. . . . I mean . . . I mean, it was bad . . . it was hard. I'm sorry. Growing up, I wasn't as emotional about it as I am now. I was so young, I didn't understand. Now I understand the loss better, and I know for sure the pain she must have been in. Though I was only four years old, I could see that she was not well. Ten minutes before she died, she assured me that she would be okay. I remember that conversation clearly. One minute she was talking to me, then ten minutes later she was gone. Yeah. We buried her in an unmarked grave nearby.

So many people lost their loved ones that day to that no-name illness. I wasn't the only one. I lost my mom, and some people lost ten, five family members.

A NEW BEGINNING

Once the U.N. discovered what happened in Burundi, they started searching for survivors. That's how we were found. Out of nowhere, U.N. trucks arrived and began picking up survivors in the forest. We were saved. We were driven far, far away, hours and hours away; it seemed like hundreds of miles from Burundi, to a protected area in Tanzania that was set up by the U.N. The name of the camp was Mtendeli, Mtendeli Refugee Camp Tanzania.

In one word, the refugee camp sucked. It was brand-new, and new refugee camps suck. People think of new things as being good, but when it comes to a refugee camp, no. Not good. The U.N. had just taken charge of the area, and there was little time to break it in. There were no roads, no running water, no left, no right. We were brought to this nothing place in the middle of the jungle and given tents. Whole families, large families, lived in one tent. There were over seventy thousand families at this camp. Seventy thousand *families,* not people.

In the beginning, we just got the necessities, blankets and stuff like that. After one year, we had streets. A year after that, we had a hospital. Two years after that, we had schools. In three years, we had markets where people could exchange and buy things. Tanzanians came to the camp to exchange goods. The area had taken shape. We were organized. There was a sense of harmony. Five years after we arrived, churches were built. By that point, we were living in brick houses. We had youth centers where we kids could go and play games. Foreigners from Europe and the United States visited. They taught us new games. We were like a village.

Many people who lived in the camp had prior professions. Some had been teachers. Others, like my sister Veronica and her husband, Justin, had been doctors. The U.N. hired them to work in the refugee camp.

Veronica was twenty-seven at that time. She and Justin had just started their medical careers at a big, beautiful hospital in Burundi run by Médecins Sans Frontières [Doctors Without Borders]. The camp hired both of them as doctors for the huge sum of eighteen dollars a month. And with that money, in that refugee camp, they could easily support us all.

The U.N. gave us food: rice, flour, beans, corn. We cooked at home. While my sister and her husband worked in the hospital, we took care of the house. Boys would do the physical things mostly. My brother Balthazar and I would go out in the bushes and gather firewood. We would gather water, drinking water and cooking water. The girls mostly would do the household chores and stuff.

A child is a child no matter where he lives. We lived in Block A, Second Street. In the evenings, the kids played tag and ran around, just like any other kids.

Two years after we moved into the camp, my dad was not doing well. He was still mourning his wife, our mom. Once he was this big-time farmer who could get anything he wanted, get any food he wanted. In the refugee camp, we ate the same food Monday through Sunday — morning, afternoon, and night. There were no options in a refugee camp; there was no future, and my dad was used to being his own man.

One day he told us, "I'm going back to Burundi. You kids stay here. It will be easier for me to dodge bullets and hide alone. I'm going to Burundi and live on my farm." He knew that he would not be bothered, because he was Hutu. We kids could still be in danger because, remember, we are mixed Hutu and Tutsi.

When my dad left the camp, Veronica and Justin became like our parents. They saved the money they got working as camp doctors and were able to build a house with a roof and everything. The soil at the back of our tent was clay, so we made bricks to build the house. We put a large tent over the house for waterproofing, and we put palm leaves on the roof to cool it down. There were chairs — no sofas, obviously — but we made beds from branches and stuff. Every three or four years, the U.N. gave us new bedding.

We didn't have a TV, but we knew about it. There were movie theaters in the community centers, but nothing that you can imagine. It was just a twenty-seven-inch TV in a room. Entertainment was an expensive luxury, and our family didn't have the money to see these shows. When I was ten years old, my friends and I decided to make our own TV show. We built a little hut, put plastic on the window, added a candle behind the plastic, and played shadows for the other kids on the block. That was amazing. We began collecting payments, candies and things. The kids had a great time. We had a great time. We made up plays and designed characters. The most famous characters were the fighting heroes, Bruce Lee, Jackie Chan, and those iconic Chinese kung fu movies that we saw at the community center. We would carve their pictures from empty cartons, put them on sticks, and play them like puppets.

We lived this life for thirteen years. I started first grade in that camp. Schools followed the Rwandan education system: primary school was from first to sixth grade, and secondary school was from seventh to twelfth grade. After twelfth grade, well, obviously we didn't have universities there, but there was a kind of technical school. Although we were in Tanzania, we followed our own cultural heritage and were taught in French.

When I was in the fifth grade, groups from countries such as the United States, Canada, and Australia started coming to the camp, looking for people to be resettled. We signed up for the U.S. and started the immigration process soon thereafter.

It was a long, long process. It took about five years to be vetted. First, they interviewed us individually, and then as a family; that is, everyone living in our house. We had to make a case about why we couldn't go back to our birth country. "What happened to you? Why do you fear going back?" We had a strong case. It probably helped that we were of mixed heritage and that my sister and brother-in-law were doctors. We waited. And we waited.

In Burundi, secondary school is a big deal. It's almost like a college degree. Not many people in my country get to go to college or university, so secondary school is important. We all take a special test the same day, same time. This is to avoid cheating or any other discrepancies. Probably this compared to the ACT [American College Testing] or SAT [Scholastic Aptitude Test] for high schools here.

When I reached sixth grade, I took the special test. I passed it with the highest score in the whole camp. (I guess I used to be smart.) I was so excited. I decided to go back to Burundi to tell my father that I was going to secondary school. I wanted him to know what I had accomplished. My friends helped me contact professional smugglers who would walk me to Burundi. It would take all night and all day to reach the border. Then it would be another six or seven hours to reach my town.

The Tanzanians had this bad habit of robbing the refugees who went outside the refugee camp. Once someone was away from the protected area, they became fair game. If you are caught outside the camp, they could do anything to you, including kill you. Even a kid five years old can stop you and say, like, "What's your name? Where you from? Where are you going?" We heard about people burned alive. We had no voice in Tanzania. No power. You must be fearless or crazy to cross on foot to the area that leads to Burundi.

In one town the smugglers and I were recognized. Tanzanians can smell Burundians. They recognized us by our clothes and mannerisms. My first fear was: I don't want to be burnt.

Luckily, they just robbed us of everything we had. I had a small stereo/radio almost the size of a phone. That was a gift I got from the school for my top grades and stuff. Obviously I wanted to show it off to my father. They took that. I also had a thousand Tanzanian shillings. A thousand Tanzanian shillings is probably under a U.S. dollar. They took them too. But they let us go and we continued with the journey.

When we got to my old village, I saw some refugee camp friends who had returned to Burundi the year before. I asked them to take me to my dad's house because I had forgotten where it was. "Oh, it's Friday," one friend said. "He might be at the local bar. That's your dad's favorite spot."

We went downtown to the local bar. Inside, there was a long bench filled with many men drinking and talking. I thought he must be here. I'll just go and surprise my dad. "Hey, surprise!" I looked at everybody there but didn't see him.

The last time I saw my father, I was about six years old. Now I was twelve. My dad was sitting right there, and I didn't recognize him. And he didn't recognize me.

I had obviously grown. As I was leaving, the man sitting next to him said to him, "Is that your son? The one who was here a year ago?"

"No. I don't think so. I don't think he'd be coming back so soon."

"But that young man looks just like him."

My father got up and followed me. As soon as I turned around, there he was, my father, right behind me. "You're so tall," he said to me.

"You're so old," I said to him. We hugged. I think we hugged for a good ten minutes. We cried. We were glued to each other. There was much catching up to do.

My father introduced me to my stepmother and three half-siblings. It was right for him to have somebody; I didn't want him to be alone. My father had been a very loving man to my mom. He was a genuine, loving man. He was my idol. I wanted to be like him when I married. My stepmom is great. She's loving and quiet. She's soft-spoken, which is very unique for our outspoken, fun, and crazy family. I cherish my half-sister and two half-brothers.

Our house had been burnt by the bad guys after they found out that we had escaped. They destroyed a lot of stuff on our property. My dad was trying to rebuild the house. Once my family and I were in America, and working, we offered to move him into the city. He was, like, "Nope, no, thank you." He was happy on his own land. I stayed with my father for a week before heading back to the refugee camp. He was thrilled to learn I aced the national test and was going on to high school.

JOY

Five years after we had begun the immigration process, we got a letter of acceptance. That was the most joyful moment that we had ever, ever had. My sister and her husband were the ones who got the letter, but it was for our entire household. By now, Victoria and Justin had three kids: Sheila, Nagrasia, and little Patrick. All the siblings who lived in the household, my brother Balthazar, and me were included in the letter. My two other sisters, Virginia and Suazis, were married and each living with their husbands' families, so they were not considered in our family anymore. They signed up for resettlement and participated the same way we did, but immigration turned them down. Many people were turned down. I don't understand this. Why did some get no, and others get yes? This is a mystery to me. Everybody had a strong story in the refugee camp. You would think that my sisters' stories were closest to ours. You would imagine they would take everybody, but no, they did not.

By 2006, there was some stability in Burundi. The U.N. decided to close the camp. The U.N. based their decision on the fact that there was no active militia fighting. But the rebel group had not yet signed a peace treaty with the government. Many refugees moved from our camp to another one because they were afraid to return to Burundi. Virginia, Suazis, and their families, for example, did not feel safe in Burundi. Rather than return home, they decided to go to a different refugee camp in Malawi. They are still in Malawi.

Seven hundred people from our refugee camp were accepted by the United States. There was pure joy. It was an unforgettable night. Unforgettable. By 2006, I was a few months shy of seventeen and about to have a new life in a place called the United States. We had no idea how we were going to get there. We had no idea how far away it was. All we knew was that it was a place somewhere out there. It had to be a hundred million times better than where we were now. Think of it this way: When we think of heaven, we know it is something good. But we can't paint it. We can't imagine whether it would be green, yellow, grassy, floating on the clouds. We don't know anything about it, but we know that it's good. Right? That's how we thought of America. It was like heaven.

16
Heaven

We learned that we would be living in an area with white people. I had seen white people who came with the U.N. When they came to our camp, kids would rush to them, to touch them, just to see if they felt like we feel. We touched their hair to see if it felt different from ours. Sometimes the volunteers would hang out with us kids. At first, it was a shock to get close to one. Even their eyes, their eyes looked like a cat. A cat's eyes. They were so unreal to us.

We learned a few things about the United States, like how to call 911 in case of an emergency. We were taught to respond to a question by saying, "No English." That was all the English we were taught. It's funny, isn't it? Once we were here, Americans would come up to me, and say, "Oh, we're so excited to have you here." And I'd respond, "No English," and look away. It was bad!

We thought that we would be taken to a protected area like our camp. We had the mind-set of a refugee. We didn't know that we were going to live in a larger society.

On August 11, 2006, we were taken to the airport in big, nice buses, for a flight to Nairobi [in Kenya]. We didn't have much to take with us, because we never had much in the first place. At the airport, I saw helicopters for the first time. We had seen airplanes in the sky but never helicopters. They made so much noise and caused so much wind. It was magical.

We waited for our turn to board the airplane. Once we sat down in our seats, something funny happened. The flight attendants started handing us plastic bags. We looked inside them. They were empty. We were, like, "Wait a minute. Are you supposed to be giving us something here? These bags are empty." As refugees, we were used to being given stuff. For such a trip, I thought we'd score big. But the bags were empty. People started complaining, like, "These bags are empty. What's going on?"

The person giving out the bags said, "Oh, those are just in case you throw up." And you know, once we lifted off, many people did throw up. Thank God, I did not.

We flew to Nairobi and were given medical examinations just to be sure that everybody was healthy. For the last five years, as part of the immigration process, we had been given routine blood tests, physical tests, and interviews. This was to be our last set of tests.

Four days later, on August 15, 2006, we boarded a second plane, heading to the United States. The first stop was Chicago. Once we landed in Chicago, everybody had their own destination cities to go to. I didn't know that we families were not going to live together.

As we walked through the terminal, going to our final boarding destinations, families began to disappear. I looked to my right, a family was gone. I looked to my left, another family gone. Walking, walking, walking, walking, walking. It seemed like people just disappeared. No one was even saying goodbye, because they probably didn't know what was happening either. What's going on? What's happening to them? I thought this to myself. I didn't say anything out loud because the only words I could say were "No English."

We went to our terminal and boarded the plane to take us to Omaha, Nebraska. By now, we were just one single family, and we were terrified. Like, "What the heck happened to everybody?" Nobody told us what was going to happen today. We felt fear. We were so scared. When we landed in Omaha, it was one a.m.

OMAHA, NEBRASKA

The city looked so beautiful. It was the first time we landed at nighttime and in an area where there were electric lights. Everything was so bright. The refugee resettlement agency that was to meet us was the Lutheran Family Services. Lacey and Jeff, who work for the agency, were waiting to greet us. Lacey was the first person to welcome us in Omaha. It was amazing.

I wish we had other Burundians to welcome us as well. But Lacey was there, and she was so good. She had already memorized our names, everybody's. "Oh, Victoria. Hi, Justin. Hello, Balthazar. Dieudonné, welcome. Welcome. Welcome."

We felt so good. We felt welcomed. Despite all the fear we had had, like, coming in and not knowing where everybody was going, and no English, we felt like we were home.

We drove down Dodge Street, one of Omaha's main streets. The streets were wide, so big, and the buildings were tall. To someone coming from a refugee camp, a five-story building was big. Right? I looked up, and said, "New York?" And Lacey and Jeff just looked at me and laughed. In preparation for the move, I had seen pictures of New York in magazines and newspapers. When I saw such tall buildings in real life, I thought this meant New York. We drove to our first home, and that's where everything really got started. Later, we learned that the Lutheran Family Services volunteers had spent months planning and setting up this house for us.

First, Lacey and Jeff showed us what a light switch does. Magic! Yeah, it was magic. They opened the refrigerator. Refrigerator? Then they showed us our microwave. What the heck? Microwave? What is this? We had never had such a thing in the refugee camp. As doctors for Médecins Sans Frontières, my sister and brother-in-law were used to all this stuff, but they were not up to the level of the technology that we had here in our very own home. In the refugee camp, the hospitals were run by generators. They only had basic things, like lights.

Lacey and Jeff had already prepared a meal for us. I don't think they knew about Burundi cooking, because we were the first Burundi family here in Omaha. They prepared roast chicken. Chicken is very common good food in Burundi. I mean, everybody eats chicken, right? That was a smart choice.

In the refugee camp, the bathroom had been outside. Now it was inside. We had been told about these things but to see it . . . to see it . . . to be in it . . . amazing. We changed from getting our water outside the house to running water inside the house. Wait! You can have the hot water and the cold water come out from the same tube? How does that happen? Everything was just magical for us. We were like little kids all over again.

Lacey and Jeff did a very good job. The following weeks, they visited us on a regular basis. Probably they wanted to be sure that we hadn't burned down the house. Really, though, they wanted to make sure that we're doing okay. They tried to help us. We constantly put the wrong food in the refrigerator and left the right food out of the refrigerator. They would put everything where it belonged, and then we would rearrange it again.

Now my wife laughs at me when I tell her about this, because she's from in the city, where they have running water and refrigerators. She was born and raised in Pointe-Noire, the Republic of the Congo.

It was way hard to relearn the whole societal structure. The society, the community, and the language were all new to us. It was like being born again. But we were old. We were being born old.

We connected to very good people. A lot of volunteers came to our house to show us where the market was, where the streets go, where the bus stop is, where the bus goes. We ate with them. We grew up Catholic. We had been baptized, gone through First Communion, all that stuff. They took us to their churches, and we worshipped together.

Six days after we arrived, school started. A volunteer took me to a high school where they tested me to determine which grade to start. I'm like, "No English! No English!" That was not the right answer.

Even though I was sixteen, even though I got the highest grade in the refugee camp, they put me back to the ninth grade. None of my secondary school time counted, because the refugee camp was on a different system, the French system. I spoke French well, but no English. The only thing I could handle was science. Science is the same wherever you go. I didn't understand math because the terminology is different. The French system uses meters and kilometers, grams and kilograms. The American system uses yards, miles, ounces, and pounds. The American system didn't make sense to me. I had to convert everything. I had to translate words. It took me longer than the other students to understand the lessons.

I was not angry about being left back. I mean, I didn't know what to expect. The language was not there. The culture was not there. I did not know how things worked. I didn't know the system. It felt normal for me to go back. I really kind of liked it because it gave me a chance to get a strong foundation.

The school they put me into had a program called ESL, English as a Second Language. I had a phenomenal teacher. Her name is Miss Gandel, Linda Gandel. She transforms students. Our classroom was diverse. We had Asians, South Americans, Africans, all in one class. We not only didn't speak English; we didn't speak each other's languages. To communicate, we would point at things. It was chaotic. Somehow Miss Gandel worked through the chaos.

I met a young man from West Africa. Yannick, from Burkina Faso. He was the only other person in the school who spoke French. We bonded. He showed me the classrooms and hallways and offices. We became best friends. We are still best friends. We invite one another to each other's parties and things like that. Miss Gandel became my friend too. She lives in the countryside, and I've visited her many times. For the last few years, she and her family have invited me to their Thanksgiving dinner.

For the entire first month, we were excited and happy. Then reality hit. We realized that we didn't know anything. We couldn't get from A to B alone. That's when the *uh-oh* feeling came in. Wait! How we gonna do this? How we gonna do that? We can't speak in English. We can't ask questions. We didn't know how to get to the market alone. And what happened to the people that we came with? We didn't even know where they went, whether they are okay or whether they're not okay. WHAT ARE WE GONNA DO HERE??? What the *heck* are we doing here? Anxiety crept into our bodies. We felt so lonely. We couldn't talk to anyone, not even our neighbors. Everything was shockingly new. But we also realized that there was no going back. We may as well cope by learning and moving forward. And we did.

My sister and brother-in-law quickly learned that their medical experiences and their degrees didn't transfer here. They could no longer work as doctors. My sister found a job as a maid in a hotel. My brother-in-law went to work in a meatpacking plant. They went to school at night to get their CNAs, Certified Nursing Assistant degrees. My brother-in-law Justin still works in a meatpacking plant so that my sister Victoria can continue school to become a full-time nurse.

There's a ten-year difference between me and my brother Balthazar. He was too old to go to high school, so he went to the Job Corps to get a GED. Job Corps is for older kids to get schooled. Once he got his GED, he studied carpentry. He loved working as a carpenter, but it was not a year-round job. He found a second job, operating a machine that makes seed bags for farmers. He's been doing that for years.

By the end of the first semester, I was communicating in English well enough to move to a regular English class. I was reading Shakespeare and stories like *The Scarlet Letter*. Although I didn't really understand 90 percent of it, I was trying. By the end of the first year in regular English class, I was getting satisfactory grades and could move on to the next class. I'm still learning, even today. I run into a word that I don't understand. Every day is a learning opportunity for me.

Many volunteers helped us. They came to the house with clothing and food. They invited us to their churches for worship. There was one church called Coram Deo. It was nondenominational, very new, started by a group of college students. They were all white Americans. They were part of the group who volunteered at Lutheran Family Services. Their pastor, his name is J.D. Senkbile, helped us get settled. I will never forget his generosity. He would come by to see how we were doing, drive us around so that we could become familiar with the city, drive us around during the holiday season to see the Christmas lights. Those were special moments that we will never forget. We agreed to visit his church even though we were already going to a Catholic church. For the first few months, when we went on our own to the Catholic church, no one noticed us. No one said, "Hello" or "Hi" or "You look confused" or "What's your name?" We didn't know the language. We stood when the congregation stood, and we sat when the congregation sat. Basically we understood what was happening because the hymns are the same — just in a different language.

When we went to J.D.'s church, it didn't look like the beautiful cathedral that felt so heavenly. It was in the back of a coffee shop. There were only about fifteen white people drinking coffee. We were, like, jeez, what is this? People are so chill in this church; they are just kicking it with a coffee mug. They crossed their legs. They prayed with coffee mugs in their hands. We were, like, this is a church? We were confused. But as soon as we got into that group, we could feel their love and their enthusiasm. They wanted to know who we are, and where we came from.

More and more Burundians were immigrating to Omaha and wanted to know where to go to church. We told them about the church, and they started coming too. Eventually Balthazar reconnected with a girl we had known back in the refugee camp. She went to college at the University of Nebraska at Omaha. She had just graduated with a bachelor's degree in human resources, minoring in marketing. They married and are living not far from us.

I met my future wife through my sister-in-law. Yes, I must give my sister-in-law the credit. Rheine had been going to college here too, studying to be a pharmacist. To make extra money, she spent time braiding women's hair, and that's how she met my sister-in-law.

One day, my sister-in-law said, "Dieu, I have someone I want you to meet."

I'm like, "Do you?"

"Yeah."

The first day I saw Rheine, I knew she was the one. We connected very, very fast. We share a lot in common. She's the last kid in her family. I'm the last kid in my family. We're both goofy. We can get goofy, but we know when to stop and get serious. We share so many things in common, especially music. We both love music.

Dieudonné attended Iowa Western Community College, a two-year school. Once he graduated, he continued his studies at the University of Nebraska Omaha, majoring in business administration. College is expensive. He still has a year to go to graduate. Meanwhile, he started working in a bank, and then he switched jobs to be a credit-card dispute agent for PayPal.

Here I am in America. I'm getting a good education, I have a good job, and I'm in love with a beautiful woman, my wife, who will soon be the mother of our son. I'm so lucky. There was one more thing I needed to do.

Rheine

Rheine and Dieudonné in front of their house

17
Umoja

Dieudonné understood from his own experiences just how challenging the transition from an African refugee camp to a modern city like Omaha can be. Some parents were having a hard time adjusting to American culture and norms, especially when it came to disciplining their children.

Dieudonné says, "In Africa, children knew that if they did something wrong, they'd get a whipping. Whipping a child was normal. That's not how kids are disciplined in the States." Young African refugee kids, nine-, ten-, twelve-year-olds, quickly adapted to the ways of this country. "Oh, I'm in America now. You can't whip me anymore. You can't punish me, or I'll call the police." In fact, some kids did call the police on their own parents. They

started disrespecting their parents. And they started getting into trouble. The
parents, working two, three, jobs in a foreign country, in a foreign language,
were having a very hard time.

The culture clash in our small community was getting out of hand. What could we do? How could we help? My friend Jack and I tried to figure out a way to help. We should distract the kids. Yes! That's it! We will distract them from the negative things going on in their heads. We will distract them into becoming good kids. And that's how we began a kids' choir.

After school, we gathered a group of kids, took them to the basement of one of our houses, and began singing their favorite songs. There was no keyboard, but we did have a drum.

While we were singing, we incorporated the teachings about our culture that related to their current lives. We read passages in the Bible, discussed them, and sang more songs. We needed to show the kids that while there are good things here in America, we must not forget where we came from.

We didn't know if this would work, but at least it was worth a try.

It was pretty fun. They love music. They love to sing. They love to dance. While we sang and danced, we embraced the values in our culture.

We didn't tell the parents what we were doing, because we didn't want the kids to find out that we had an agenda. As far as the parents were concerned, their kids were attending a choir.

Choir rehearsal

As far as we were concerned, we were counseling them on how to combine the new culture with the old culture.

Tupendane,
   tupendane.

(Let's love each other, let's love each other.)

After about three, four months, the parents began calling us. "Dieudonné, what exactly did you do to my child?" I worried. Did I do something wrong? The parents told me that their son or daughter was coming home from school, doing homework, washing dishes. They cleaned the house without being asked to do it. "What did you do?" That's when we started to feel confident. We said, "It's just a choir."

A few months later, the parents and friends with musical backgrounds joined the choir.
Ten, fifteen families would go to someone's home and have a great time.

Tunaimba.

(We sing.)

Tunacheza.

(We dance.)

Twa toa shukurani.

(We give thanks.)

Two years later, pastor Daniel Niyonzima from a Methodist church in Iowa visited us. We knew him from the refugee camp. "You know what?" he said. "It's time to come out of the basement and move to a place where more people can gather and worship."

Our group loved the idea of a church of our own. We talked to our church leaders and explained that we wanted to start our own ministry in our own language. They were very understanding. The Saint Paul Methodist church gave us a large space in their building and we were on our way.

The Welengo family

In the last three years, refugees from different African countries arrived in Omaha—the Congo, Rwanda, Kenya. We welcomed the refugees. Swahili was a language that united all of us. For those people who do not speak Swahili, some congregants act as Kirundi translators. In our church, there is *no English*.

Aziza and Roger Bwarni

Jumuiya moja.

(We are a community.)

Deogratias and Josephine Basekokariyo

We teach the new folks how to drive. We help them with their driving test. We carpool before they get their own cars.

The Waciba family

We help them find jobs. Many of us work in the meatpacking plants, a job available to refugees regardless of their language skills. Helping each other find jobs lightens the burden of the resettlement agency.

Rheine and Dieudonné Manirakizas

We have become the religious and social center of our community. We call ourselves the Umoja Choir. *Umoja* means "unity" or "united." That's what we are.

Umoja.

(United.)

PART VI

NOTES
AND
RESOURCES

The Refugee Process

HOW REFUGEES ARE RESETTLED IN AMERICA

The United Nations High Commissioner for Refugees (UNHCR) reports that "We are now witnessing the highest level of displacement on record. An unprecedented 68.5 million people around the world have been foreced from home." At this writing, fifty-seven percent of the refugees come from three countries: Afghanistan, South Sudan, and Syria. Over half of them are under the age of eighteen.

In the United States, offering safe haven to people fleeing war, persecution, natural disasters, and other intolerable conditions is a time-honored practice. The president, in consultation with Congress, annually accepts a specific number of refugees. The process for admitting these refugees is lengthy, arduous, and complicated. Many government and nongovernmental organizations (NGOs) work hand in hand to resettle individuals and families from refugee camps to new homes in the United States. Only the UNHCR, a U.S. Embassy, or certain NGOs may refer a refugee for resettlement. Then the vetting process begins. Here are the steps:

1. The refugee is initially screened by the UNHCR. Biodata (names, addresses, date and place of birth, etc.) and biometrics (iris scans) are collected and first interviews are conducted. Only the strongest candidates for resettlement — about 1 percent — advance to the next step.

2. The UNHCR sends its recommendations and referrals to the Resettlement Support Center (RSC). The RSC performs administrative and processing functions, including collecting biographical data and preparing the candidate's file.

3. Security agencies in the United States — the National Counterterrorism Center, the FBI, the Department of Homeland Security (DHS), and the State Department — review the materials gathered by the RSC.

4. Officers from the United States Citizenship and Immigration Services (USCIS), a division of the Department of Homeland Security, travel to the country where the refugee is currently living to conduct additional extensive interviews, do background checks, and retake fingerprints and biometric data. The fingerprints are sent to the FBI, DHS, and the U.S. Department of Defense databases for enhanced screening. At the time this book was written, the entire process usually took between eighteen months and two years.

5. The refugee undergoes medical testing for tuberculosis and certain venereal diseases.

6. Once all the steps above are completed, the refugee is assigned to one of nine private nongovernmental organizations that work with the federal government:

> Church World Service (CWS)
> Ethiopian Community Development Council (ECDC)
> Episcopal Migration Ministries (EMM)
> Hebrew Immigrant Aid Society (HIAS)
> International Rescue Committee (IRC)
> U.S. Committee for Refugees and Immigrants (USCRI)
> Lutheran Immigration and Refugee Services (LIRS)
> United States Conference of Catholic Bishops (USCCB)
> World Relief (WR)

These agencies then take over the resettlement process. The nine agencies oversee about 250 affiliates — groups such as the Lutheran Family Services of Nebraska — that manage the U.S. portion of the journey.

7. The refugee attends cultural orientation classes.

8. The affiliate agency determines the best location for resettlement and makes the travel arrangements. Before the refugee can travel to the United States, there is one more screening by the U.S. Customs and Border Protection Agency.

9. Once the refugee arrives in the States, representatives from the affiliate greet the refugee at the airport and arrange housing, schooling, and other essential services as described by the participants in *In Search of Safety*. Because the refugee typically arrives with very few possessions, the federal government provides the local organizations with a small amount of financial assistance. The assistance is to cover expenses for the refugee's food, housing, employment, medical care, counseling, and other services for ninety days. After the ninety days, the refugee is expected to have a job and pay taxes.

According to the International Rescue Committee, "Refugees must rebuild their lives from traumatic and tragic circumstances. The majority embrace their newly adopted homeland with tremendous energy and success. They go on to work, attend universities, build professions, purchase homes, raise children, and contribute to their communities. Ultimately, refugees obtain citizenship and become fully participating members of society. They become Americans."

HOW A REFUGEE BECOMES A CITIZEN

A refugee is immediately entitled to work in the United States. The U.S. Citizen and Immigration Services website states that "refugees receive Form I-94 containing a refugee admission stamp. Additionally, a Form I-765, Application for Employment Authorization, will be filed . . . in order . . . to receive an Employment Authorization Document (EAD)." While the refugees wait for their EAD authorization, they can use their Form I-94, also known as their Arrival-Departure Record, as proof of permission to work in the United States. After one year, the refugee is required to apply for a green card, which allows all immigrant residents the right to live and work permanently in the United States. (Applying for a green card sets off another round of security vetting.) Lawful permanent residents are eligible to seek U.S. citizenship after living in the United States for five years. They must be able to read and write basic English, pass a test on U.S. history and government, establish that they have good moral character and are committed to uphold the U.S. Constitution, and swear an oath of allegiance to the United States. (Applying for citizenship also activates another round of security vetting.)

SOURCES

Felter, Claire, and James McBride. "How Does the U.S. Refugee System Work?" Council on Foreign Relations website. Updated October 10, 2018. https://www.cfr.org/backgrounder/how-does-us-refugee-system-work.

Pope, Amy. "Infographic: The Screening Process for Refugee Entry into the United States." The White House website/President Barack Obama archives. November 20, 2015. https://obamawhitehouse.archives.gov/blog/2015/11/20/infographic-screening-process-refugee-entry-united-states.

United Nations High Commissioner for Refugees. "Global Trends: Forced Displacement in 2016." UNHCR website. June 19, 2017. https://www.unhcr.org/globaltrends2016/.

United States Citizenship and Immigration Services. "Refugees." U.S. Citizenship and Immigration Services website. Accessed December 4, 2018. https://www.uscis.gov/humanitarian/refugees-asylum/refugees.

United States Department of State. "Bureau of Population, Refugees, and Migration: 2017 Global Funding and Projects." U.S. Department of State website. October 17, 2017. https://www.state.gov/j/prm/releases/factsheets/2017/274859.htm.

Author's Note

This book is personal. My grandparents' stories about harrowing flights from Russia and Ukraine to Philadelphia, Pennsylvania, are somewhat similar to some of the stories featured in *In Search of Safety*. When my ancestors left home, they knew that they would never again see the country of their birth. Never again would they see their parents, aunts, and uncles. Meyer, my maternal grandfather, told me that the night he reached Paris, he cried so hard his entire pillow was soaked through. Their accounts about arriving in a country where they did not know the language, culture, or traditions are deeply rooted in my being. They had no professional skills and no money. And yet they came — wide-eyed, idealistic, and looking toward a successful future. I loved hearing my grandparents' stories. I was inspired by the way they turned nothing but their wits, will, and grit into successful lives. There is a direct line between my conversations with the five individuals featured in this book and those I had as a girl during long drives and blissful walks with my grandfather in Philadelphia's Fairmount Park. *In Search of Safety* is my way of saying thank you to my ancestors.

Even though I live in a city, New York, where many refugees make their first stop, it took me a long time to get this book started. Contacting the refugees was far more complicated than I had imagined it would be. Some people wanted to tell their stories, but their experiences were too raw, too tormented, to relive. Some people did not want their lives revealed publicly but felt an obligation to the caring mentors and volunteers who helped them establish a new life in a safe country. Those folks needed to be let off the hook. Most organizations, overworked, understaffed, and definitely underpaid, lacked the bandwidth to add another project to their calendar. There were many ups and downs, starts and stops, before the book found its home in the middle of the country: Nebraska.

Nebraska, the state of my husband's birth and youth, is my "in-law state." The spirit of Willa Cather's rugged pioneers exists there to this day. Nebraska turns out to be an excellent destination for refugees. Jobs are plentiful, and housing is affordable. In Nebraska, the refugee is welcomed.

My supportive and sympathetic Omaha sister-in-law Bonnie Kuklin Horwich was instrumental in helping me establish the necessary connections. She spoke with her rabbi, Steven Abraham of Beth El Synagogue, about my difficulty finding refugees who were willing to be interviewed. Rabbi Abraham referred Bonnie to Lutheran Family Services, a well-known and highly respected volunteer organization. He called the program development officer, Lacey Studnicka, and she in turn introduced me to the individuals whose stories are featured in this book and to directors of additional organizations that played a part in *In Search of Safety*.

It's impossible not to smile when in the company of Lacey. During our first meeting, she mentioned that volunteers were very busy because a new Afghani family was arriving in a few days. This mostly faith-based group of volunteers were rushing around town shopping to get an apartment ready for the newcomers. She asked if I'd like to come to the airport for the welcoming. "Are you kidding?" I said. "Absolutely!"

When it came to finding a representative mix of willing refugees, Lacey got it. She would call, saying, "Have I got a rock star for you!" She introduced us via phone calls and e-mails and then stepped back so that the refugee would be comfortable saying no. Some did. And that was perfectly understandable. But five people said yes, so a book began to take shape. Traveling back and forth to Nebraska was an enjoyable experience because of Bonnie's organizing skills and hospitality. The refugee experience is an enormous subject, and *In Search of Safety* was not able to include every piece of the resettlement process. Instead, it simply introduces five special individuals so that you, the reader, can experience what it is like to be caught up in and escape from a deadly situation beyond one's control. It is a reminder of human beings' undaunting will to survive, adjust, and thrive.

I am honored to know Fraidoon, Nathan, Nyarout, Shireen, and Dieudonné. It has been a pleasure to spend time with them and their families. They have received many gifts from their newly adopted country. And in return they've given back in many ways. My life is certainly richer for knowing them.

May we not forget that there are many more people still waiting in refugee camps, still risking dangerous journeys, and still making long treks in search of safety. May we not forget that those who wait have much to contribute. May they be welcomed to safe havens everywhere.

Acknowledgments

First, last, and forever, I am so grateful to Fraidoon Akhtari, Nathan Htoo, Nyarout Majiok, Shireen Jardo Al-Hanto, and Dieudonné Manirakiza. Their friends' and families' contributions were also invaluable: Homa, Fradin, and Leema Akhtari; Sari M. Long; David Lemoine; the Htoo family: Billy, Eh Ku, Hel But Say, Helblu L Htoo, Helblu L Say, and Hei Blut Laura Paw; David Majiok, Nyarout and her children, Nyagoa, Nyabima, Emanuel, Ajeal, and Bukjiok; and Rheine Manirakiza.

Thank you to the staff and volunteers at the Lutheran Family Services of Nebraska, Inc., including Lacey Studnicka, LFS's director of advancement; Ruth Henrich, president and CEO; Todd Reckling, vice president of programming; Mosah Goodman, vice president of legal and support services; and Jennifer Gentle, volunteer coordinator. This book could not have been written without them.

Thank you, Malikal Goak, director of Caring People Sudan. While fielding numerous phone calls from anxious and desperate people in South Sudan, Malikal counseled me about the history and political climate of his country. Malikal also introduced me to Nyarout and her family.

When we met, Shireen did not speak English. But one did not have to know Kurmanji to understand the suffering and anguish in her words. As of this writing, she still does not know what happened to eighteen members of her family. It is her hope that someone will read her story here and rescue them. Hadi Pir, who served as an interpreter for the U.S. Army in Iraq and is currently vice president of the Yazda Cultural Center (in Lincoln, Nebraska), was the translator during the long, emotional interview with Shireen. Hadi also provided invaluable background information about Yazidi culture and history. Jolene McCulley, the center's program manager, gave up her office so that we could record privately. She also provided additional contextual material about the Yazidi population in Nebraska. Saad Babir worked on the translation of the recordings. Laila Khoudeika graciously translated my questions and Shireen's answers throughout the long editing process. She provided additional material from Shireen's visa application. Laila Hesso, who has given Shireen a warm and caring home, helped translate last-minute questions throughout the editing process. Thank you all.

Soon after the last photographs were taken for this book, Dieudonné and Rheine Manirakiza became parents of a baby boy, Davin. With loving parents like the Manirakizas, Davin will live a happy and beautiful life. Thank you for sharing your story and for giving Nebraska the spectacular choir Umoja. Thank you, congregants and ministers of the African Ministry, for so graciously allowing me to photograph your choir rehearsal and services.

Fraidoon and Shireen generously provided their personal photographs. Kathleen Anderson at the International Center for Photography (ICP) helped tweak and print the photographs. I learn so much every time we are together.

Many people encouraged me and tried to help me kick-start this book: the Very Reverend Patrick Keating, deputy chief executive officer of Catholic Charities, Diocese of Brooklyn; Professors Johnathan Weiner and Gary Sick at Columbia University; Toby Volkman; Lucia Zerner; Carolyn Ward; Shelly Cryer; and Riham Alkousaa. All took time from their busy lives to help with leads, links, or descriptions of the triumphs and difficulties of the refugee experience.

A special thanks to Maryellen Fullerton and Stacy Caplow, the awe-inspiring professors of immigration law at Brooklyn Law School. Their instruction, support, and friendship throughout this journey exceeded my expectations. I have appreciated learning about immigration and refugee law from them. Thank you, Bonnie Kuklin Horwich, for not letting me give up. I'm fortunate to have you as my sister-in-law. I am deeply grateful to Rabbi Steven Abraham of Beth El Synagogue, Omaha, and to Howard Epstein, executive director of the Jewish Federation of Omaha Foundation. Without them, *In Search of Safety* would not have been.

All the participants read their sections of *In Search of Safety* for accuracy and authenticity. In addition, I am indebted to my tough, enthusiastic friends who read or offered useful counsel throughout this undertaking: law professors Bailey Kuklin, Maryellen Fullerton, and Stacy Caplow; and writers Robie Harris, Elizabeth Levy, Thea Lurie, Deborah Heiligman, Fatima Shaik and Paul O Zelinsky.

Please indulge me a few more lines to thank the people who brought *In Search of Safety* to life. Thank you, my dear agent, Brianne Johnson, at Writers House. Thank you to all at Candlewick Press for being bold, ethical, and compassionate. You give the world such notable books, and I am honored to publish with you. Hilary Van Dusen, my wise, thoughtful editor, brings a sharp eye, exquisite insight, and an empathetic heart to every page, every sentence, every word. In addition, my deepest thanks and appreciation to the best team an author could wish for:

Sherry Fatla (art director), Hayley Parker (designer), Pam Consolazio (jacket designer), Pamela Marshall and Hannah Mahoney (copyeditors), Sarah Chaffee Paris and Martha Dwyer (proofreaders), and Phoebe Kosman (publicist).

I have spent most of my adult life as a photojournalist and a nonfiction writer. These combined professions have enabled me to know people from many different cultures and walks of life. I would never have had such privileged experiences without my partner, my love, my husband, Bailey Kuklin.

Last, thank you to the generous volunteers and openhearted citizens of Nebraska.

About Lutheran Family Services of Nebraska

Every October, the president of the United States determines how many refugees will be allowed into the country for the year. Nine federally funded resettlement organizations (see page 215) distribute these refugees across the country to their nongovernmental affiliates. Lutheran Family Services (LFS) of Nebraska works with two of the nine organizations: Lutheran Immigration and Refugee Services and Church World Service.

Since 1892, Lutheran Family Services of Nebraska has assisted children and families in need. One of the many services LFS provides is to act as advocates for the immigrant community. They have resettled more refugees per capita than organizations in any other state. In fact, LFS is considered one of the most successful resettlement programs in the country, and other groups have modeled their programs after it.

The folks who work for and volunteer at LFS believe that welcoming people at dire risk to a new, safe place is an American value. The director of advancement, Lacey Studnicka, says, "People of faith are called to this job and so are ordinary citizens who just want to help. Corporate groups, book clubs, Girl Scout troops, high school classes, students from local universities, and friends and families of other volunteers step up to act as mentors to a newly arrived person.

"When a refugee family walks off the airplane, they are taken to a home that's fully functional. Volunteers help us gather furniture. They decorate. Groceries are in the fridge, clothes are in the closet, toys are on the shelves. Some items are required by law. For example, every family must have their own beds, a couch, and kitchen table and chairs. We ask our volunteers to gather both mandatory and culturally appropriate items. Volunteers are given an ethnically suitable grocery list so that they can buy the kinds of food the refugees are familiar with and may eat. Hygiene products, towels, and diapers that the family might need straightaway are in the bathroom. Will the refugees use everything right away? Maybe not. But we have everything in place before they arrive."

Volunteers greet the new arrivals at the airport. The arriving person or family has literally a "welcome wagon" of people. Lacey says, "People bring balloons and signs. We provide people who have been traveling maybe twenty-four, thirty-six hours, scared out of their minds, and not sure what the heck is going on, with a group of new friends who know their names and who carry signs of welcome. Some volunteers have asked us, 'Isn't it a little overwhelming to have so many people at the airport?' But the feedback that we've received from our refugee families is that it feels so awfully good to know that they are home, they are in a safe place, and that they are not alone."

One volunteer acts as a mentor to each newly arrived refugee family. Refugees need to know how to maneuver in a completely unfamiliar home and city. Some refugees have little education or are unskilled, and unaware of modern utilities. Their kids need to be placed in school. Doctor and dentist appointments must be set up. They need answers to lots of questions: How can one travel around town? Where's the nearest grocery store? Is there a church or mosque nearby? They need to apply for Social Security cards, green cards, and driver's licenses. Banking and credit cards have to be (sometimes) explained and also acquired. More. So much more. English-speaking volunteers teach English and other practical classes at an LFS office or do one-on-one tutoring at the refugee's home. There is also a "career and connections" mentoring program. War does not discriminate. A refugee can be a doctor (like Dieudonné's sister and brother-in-law), a lawyer, an engineer, or even a diplomat. At first, both skilled and unskilled refugees typically work as unskilled laborers or in stores like Walmart. Lacey says, "Even highly skilled refugees often work in meatpacking plants while they learn English. Once they are speaking English, we try to help find an upgrade. The career-mentoring program teams the refugee up with someone in their profession who then helps them find a path back to their careers."

LFS has its own legal services department. An immigration attorney and staff process green cards, family reunification forms, and applications for citizenship.

All federally funded refugee programs in the United States have specific requirements; all across the country, they are funded the exact same amount. As of this writing, the government gives refugees $925 per person as a one-time resettlement payment. That cash is used to pay for rent, utilities, food, and other expenses. The U.S. government expects the refugee to be self-sufficient within ninety days of arrival. Because this is not nearly enough time or money for a person or family to land on their feet, LFS has had to find ways to expand its services.

Lutheran Family Services developed a program called the International Center of the Heartland (ICH). Lacey says that because it is "privately funded, we don't have any financial restrictions. This allows us to provide ongoing case management and resources for refugees beyond the ninety days and for as long as they need help. We served five thousand people last year. Instead of telling a family that we are out of funding for them after ninety days, we can give them a new case manager through the International Center.

"Refugees who were resettled by another agency in Nebraska can also receive this service. A refugee who was resettled in another state and chooses to move to Nebraska can also receive our services. Victims of international human trafficking, a sex or labor slave, can receive our ongoing services. Our door is open to all persons seeking asylum. It's exciting to be able to do this for the community. Through the International Center, we have a robust interpreter program. There are interpreters working in twenty-six languages and dialects. If a dentist, a doctor, or another social service agency needs an interpreter for their clients, they can access one through our agency."

ABOUT LACEY STUDNICKA

Lacey is a legend among the refugee communities in Nebraska. Her enormous smile is often the first thing a refugee sees when stepping off the plane. Originally from Lincoln, Nebraska, Lacey spent a year after college in India. That trip opened her heart and expanded her mind. "When I came back," she says, "I took part in AmeriCorps, which is like the Peace Corps, working with refugees who were living in Lincoln. Once you start working with refugees, you fall in love. And then I doubly fell in love — with the man who became my husband, who's from Tajikistan. He was getting his MBA in Omaha. Fifteen years ago, we married, and I moved to Omaha. I found a job with Lutheran Family Services because I wanted to work with refugees and at the time they were the only organization doing that. Since then, I've worn many hats here. This job is special because we now have so many wonderful partners in the community who have come forward to help the refugee community."

There is not much public pushback in Omaha. Lacey says, "I truly believe that once you meet refugees and build a connection, your heart wraps around them." Lacey and Jennifer Gentle, the coordinator of volunteers, do community presentations throughout the year. Last year they gave more than two hundred addresses in churches, synagogues, mosques, and Kiwanis and Rotary clubs, among other places. Lacey says, "We've developed a small speaker's bureau of refugee folks who come with us when we do community presentations. It's the stories of the refugees that change hearts and minds. Their voices are most important. People need to hear them.

"I've done this work for a long time, and really, before the Syrian crisis, people didn't know that refugees were even here. With what was happening in Syria and with images of people coming off the boats into Europe, our community's hearts were breaking. Nebraskans would call and say, 'How can we help?' We've had volunteer families say, 'We're not going to give Christmas presents this year. Instead, we're going to sponsor a family so that our kids can go to the airport and be a part of something bigger than themselves.'" For more information about Lutheran Family Services, visit https://www.lfsneb.org/.

About the Yazda Cultural Center

In 2014, when ISIS started committing genocide against the Yazidi people, several thousand survivors came to the United States. Approximately three thousand Yazidis have settled in Lincoln, Nebraska. In time, the Yazidi community built a nonprofit center, the Yazda Cultural Center. It provides a place where Yazidi refugees can study English and learn what is expected of them in the United States. Jolene McCulley, the program manager, describes some of what the center does: "There are classes and group discussions to explain how the government works. We teach the legal system. We teach about the employment systems. We try to cover all the bases to help the newly arrived refugee understand how to live in America. The center's first goals are to help the community feel safe and hopeful and to keep their culture alive. It is only after that that we can help them learn English, learn how to apply for jobs, learn to live in an integrated community.

The center has begun a project to collect evidence of crimes against the Yazidi people before they came to the States. The researchers seek information on missing persons, such as Shireen's missing family members. They identify mass graves and the destruction of religious sites. There's a women's center to provide formerly captive and abused ISIS survivors with counseling, support, and medical attention. The cultural center also works with children and adults to "promote and protect" the Yazidi language, culture, and traditions.

Yazda has become a huge, worldwide humanitarian agency, with additional centers in Canada, Germany, Iraq, Australia, and Great Britain. In 2018, Nadia Murad, a Yazda member and a survivor of ISIS atrocities, was awarded the Nobel Peace Prize for her effort to end the use of sexual violence as a weapon of war. Her lawyer, Amal Clooney, is the legal counsel for Yazda. They, along with other members of the Yazidi community, are working to hold ISIS accountable for their crimes against humanity.

Yazda's main U.S. branches are in Lincoln and Houston. To learn more about this organization, visit https://www.yazda.org.

Chapter Notes

PART I: ARRIVE
CHAPTER 1: THE FIRST DAY OF MY LIFE

p. 8: "two fatwas against his life are still in effect": Although Fraidoon's fatwas were in fact death sentences, the definition of the word *fatwa* is far broader, referring to any legal opinion or decree handed down by an Islamic religious leader.

According to the Islamic Supreme Council of America, "In recent years, the term 'fatwā' has been widely used throughout the media, usually to indicate that a death sentence has been dealt to someone or some group of people. The limited use of this term has resulted in a limited understanding of its meaning." ("What Is a Fatwa?" Islamic Supreme Council of America, accessed December 4, 2018, http://islamicsupremecouncil.org/understanding-islam/legal-rulings/44 -what-is-a-fatwa.html.)

CHAPTER 2: FRAIDOON

p. 17: "The Mujahideen did not like the fact that my father joined . . .": The word *mujahideen* can refer to any force of Muslim warriors. The term came to be widely known in the West in reference to guerrilla fighters opposing the Soviet-backed Afghan government during the Soviet-Afghan War, from 1979 to 1989. By joining the Afghan National Army, Fraidoon's father was siding with the government, against the Mujahideen.

p. 18: "They called themselves Taliban": The Soviet Union withdrew its forces from Afghanistan in 1989, and in 1992, the Soviet-backed president was overthrown. Many areas were controlled by the Mujahideen, but the various groups weren't able to form a unified government. Into this vacuum came the Taliban, a brutal and strictly fundamentalist fighting force. See Pierre Tristam,

"History of the Taliban: Who They Are, What They Want," Thought.Co, January 24, 2018, https://www.thoughtco.com/history-of-the-taliban-who-they-are-what-they-want-2352797.

p. 18: "what we call a *madrasa*": The word *madrasa* refers to any type of educational institution, but in the West, the term is often used to refer to traditional Islamic schools.

p. 19: "sent them to fight jihad": The word *jihad* means a personal struggle or effort in devotion to Islam. It is often translated to mean a holy war waged on behalf of Islam as part of one's religious duty.

p. 19: "Their music was even in a different language, Pashto": Pashto is an Indo-European language spoken in Afghanistan, Eastern Iran, and Pakistan.

p. 20: "The enemy was the Northern Alliance, one of the Mujahideen parties": The Afghan Northern Alliance was formed by President Burhanuddin Rabbani and former defense minister Ahmad Shah Massoud. It was an armed military organization formed to fight the Taliban. The Alliance received support from Iran, Russia, Turkey, India, and Tajikistan. The Taliban were backed by Al-Qaeda.

CHAPTER 3: FRED

p. 28: "we landed inside a PRT [Provincial Reconstruction Team] run by U.S. military forces": According to the *Afghanistan Provincial Reconstruction Team Handbook,* PRTs "find their origin in coalition humanitarian liaison cells established by U.S. military forces in Operation Enduring Freedom (OEF) [the U.S. government's official name for the Global War on Terrorism] in early 2002. A dozen Army civil affairs (CA) soldiers staffed these small outposts, dubbed 'Chiclets,' with the task to assess humanitarian needs, implement small-scale reconstruction projects, and establish relations with the U.N. Assistance Mission in Afghanistan (UNAMA) and nongovernmental organizations already in the field." (United States Department of Defense/Defense Technical Information Center, *Afghanistan Provincial Reconstruction Team Handbook,* February 2011, p. 3, https://apps.dtic.mil/dtic/tr /fulltext/u2/a550604.pdf.)

CHAPTER 4: WHO WOULD MARRY SOMEONE WITH A FATWA ON HIS HEAD?

p. 40: "They were speaking Pashai, a different language . . .": Pashai (or Pashayi) is a group of languages spoken by the Pashai people in the northeast corner of Afghanistan.

p. 41: "I was back in Laghman Province, working as a linguist for the army and for the MEP company, Mission Essential Personnel": Mission Essential Personnel is a government contractor serving intelligence and military clients. It is a leading provider of translators and interpreters.

CHAPTER 5: COMING TO AMERICA, THE HARD WAY

p. 48: "SIV, Special Immigrant Visa": SIVs are granted to interpreters and others who have worked with the U.S. military in support of missions in Afghanistan and Iraq. Fraidoon's lawyer, Sari Long, provides additional information: "There is the SIV program for Iraqi and Afghan translators that is limited to fifty principal applicants per year. Since 2009, with the passage of the Afghan Allies Act, an additional SIV program was enacted for Afghans who were employed by or on behalf of the U.S. government. Initially, 7,500 visas were available for principal applicants over five years. Congress has authorized extensions over the years providing more visas. Since December 19, 2014, 14,500 visas have been allocated.

"At the time when Fred applied," she continues, "the requirement for the SIV program for Afghans was twelve months of faithful and valuable service to the U.S. government. For applicants after October 1, 2015, they must show two years of faithful and valuable service."

(See also: U.S. Department of State/Bureau of Consular Affairs, "Special Immigrant Visas for Iraqis Who Were Employed by/on Behalf of the U.S. Government," Travel.State.Gov, accessed December 4, 2018, https://travel.state.gov/content/travel/en/us-visas/immigrate /special-immg-visas-iraqis-employed-us-gov.html.)

PART II: BIRTH
CHAPTER 7: FLIP-FLOPS, RICE, SOCCER

p. 67: "The Karens (pronounced KAH-renz), the second-largest ethnic group in Myanmar . . .": It is believed that the Karen people originated in the Gobi Desert in Mongolia or in Tibet. They speak Pwo and Sgaw, two languages that are part of the Tibeto-Burman family. The Karens are governed by chiefs or princes, and they practice several religions: Buddhism, Christianity, and Islam.

p. 69: "they moved about fifty thousand of us deeper into Thailand, into one large camp called Mae La": For additional information about and photographs of this camp, see "Mae La," The Border Consortium website, accessed December 4, 2018, http://www.thebordersonsortium.org/where -we-work/camps-in-thailand/mae-la, and "Gallery of Mae La Refugee Camp," Burma Link website, accessed December 4, 2018, https://www.burmalink.org/gallery-mae-la-refugee-camp/.

p. 75: "Those who pass are eventually offered a permanent home in a third country": According to the U.N. High Commissioner for Refugees, from 2005 to 2008, the UNHCR "helped resettle more than 20,000 Myanmar refugees in Thailand — including Karens and other minority groups — in countries such as the United States, Canada, Australia, the United Kingdom, Finland, the Netherlands, New Zealand, Sweden[,] Norway . . . and Ireland." (Steven O'Brien, "It's a Long Way from Myanmar for Karen Refugees," UNHCR website, January 28, 2008, https://www.unhcr.org/afr/news/latest/2008/1/479e058f2/its-long-way-myanmar-karen-refugee%22s.html/.)

CHAPTER 8: TV, HAMBURGERS, FOOTBALL

p. 83: "to attend Karen Martyrs' Day": For more information about Karen Martyrs' Day, see various articles at the *Karen News* website: http://karennews.org/tag/karen-martyrs-day/.

p. 85: "I heard that the Susan T. Buffett Scholarship paid full college tuition for students who lived in Nebraska": See "College Scholarships," Susan Thompson Buffett Foundation, https://buffettscholarships.org.

PART III: RUN
CHAPTER 9: IN AFRICA

p. 101: "The camp collected many lost kids [who came to be known as the Lost Boys and Girls of Sudan]": For more on the lost children of Sudan, see "The Lost Boys of Sudan," International Rescue Committee website, October 3, 2014, https://www.rescue.org/article/lost-boys-sudan, and Emmanuel Nyabera, "The Lost Girls of Sudan," *Refugees* 1, No. 126 (2006), 8–9, https://www.unhcr.org/3cb5508b2.pdf.

CHAPTER 10: IN AMERICA

p. 110: "We had our I-94, a document that said we could come to U.S.": An I-94 is a "record of admission" to the United States that every noncitizen receives when entering the country. At the time Nyarout and her family arrived, the I-94 was in paper form. Visitors who were not refugees had the form stapled onto their passports when they arrived and removed when they departed. Now the process is electronic. Because refugees do not have foreign passports, the Department of Homeland Security provides I-94 forms in paper as evidence of their status and employment authorization. ("Definition of an I-94," U.S. Customs and Border Protection website, July 27, 2017, https://help.cbp.gov/app/answers

/detail/a_id/880/~/definition-of-an-i-94; "Refugee Form I-94 Automation," U.S. Citizenship and Immigration Services website, April 4, 2017, https://www.uscis.gov/i-9-central /refugee-form-i-94-automation.)

p. 119: "I finally started going to school through Job Corps": Job Corps is the largest governmental free education-and-job-training program for young adults between ages sixteen and twenty-four. More information at https://www.jobcorps.gov.

PART IV: SURVIVE
CHAPTER 11: CAPTURED

pp. 137–139: "Theirs is an ancient religion, spread orally by holy men, that is related to Zoroastrianism, Mithraism, Judaism, Christianity, and Islam": Zoroastrianism, founded by the Iranian prophet and religious reformer Zoroaster over three thousand years ago, is one of the oldest religions still practiced today. Its fundamental belief is in the presence of a supreme god, Ahura Mazda, and the struggle between his twin children Spentu Mainyu (the spirit of good) and Angra Mainyu (the spirit of evil). See "Zoroastrianism," History Channel website, August 23, 2018, https://www.history.com/topics/religion/zoroastrianism.

Mithraism is an ancient and enigmatic Persian religion that is even older than Zoro-astrianism and had a resurgence in the Roman Empire from the second to fourth centuries CE. Mithra was the Iranian god of the sun, justice, contracts, and war.

For additional information about Yazidi history and beliefs, see Avi Asher-Schapiro, "Who Are the Yazidis, the Ancient, Persecuted Religious Minority Struggling to Survive in Iraq?" *National Geographic News,* August 11, 2014, https://news.nationalgeographic.com/news /2014/08/140809-iraq-yazidis-minority-isil-religion-history.

p. 143: "A master is prohibited from having intercourse . . .": This wording is from an ISIS pamphlet that was, according to Human Rights Watch, "posted on a pro-ISIS Twitter account and generally considered authentic" and that included rules for having sex with captured and enslaved non-Muslim women and girls. (Kenneth Roth, "Slavery: The ISIS Rules," Human Rights Watch website, September 5, 2015, https://www.hrw.org/news/2015/09/05/slavery-isis-rules; see also: Rukmini Callimachi, "ISIS Enshrines a Theology of Rape," *New York Times,* August 13, 2015, https://www .nytimes.com/2015/08/14/world/middleeast/isis-enshrines-a-theology-of-rape.html.)

p. 145: "especially those who resisted reading the Quran": The term *Quran* is a transliteration from the Arabic. It can also be transliterated as *Qur'an* or *Koran.*

CHAPTER 12: FOR SALE

p. 148: "these two tiny villages were once Shiite towns . . .": Shiite (Shia) and Sunni are the two branches of Islam. As DePaul University law professor and Islamic scholar M. Cherif Bassiouni explained it, "The Sunni tradition, which today comprises approximately 85–90 percent of all Muslims, differs from Shia tradition, which comprises the remainder of the Muslim world. The distinction between the two traditions essentially derives from different approaches to governance. The Sunni believe, based on specific provisions of the Quran and the Sunna [part of Muslim law based on Muhammad's words], that the Muslim people are to be governed by consensus (ijma') through an elected head of state, the khalifa, according to democratic principles. The Shia, however, believe that the leader of Islam, whom they refer to as the imam rather than the khalifa, must be a descendant of the Prophet. The concept is the basis for a hereditary hierarchy in the Shia tradition." ("Schools of Thought in Islam," Middle East Institute website, January 24, 2012, http://www.mei.edu/publications/schools-thought-islam.)

p. 149: "She was forced to marry this militant under Sharia law": The word *Sharia,* or *Sharī'ah,* literally means "the path to a watering hole." Again as Professor M. Cherif Bassiouni has explained, "The Sharia contains the rules by which a Muslim society is organized and governed, and it provides the means to resolve conflicts among individuals and between the individual and the state." ("Islamic Law: The Shariah," Middle East Institute website, January 24, 2012, http://www.mei.edu/publications/islamic-law-shariah.)

p. 149: "During the Roji and Eda Rojiet Ezi holiday": Roji and Eda Rojiet Ezi (Fasting and Feasting) is one of the most important Yazidi holidays of the year. Participants fast from dawn to sunset for three days. After sunset, there is food, celebration, and prayer. ("Holidays," Yezidis International website, accessed December 5, 2108, http://www.yezidisinternational.org/abouttheyezidipeople/holidays.)

CHAPTER 13: THE BLACK HOLE OF CAPTIVITY

p. 164: "I kissed the hand of our spiritual leader, Baba Sheikh, as an act of respect": Baba Sheikh is the spiritual head of the Yazidis. He presides over Yazidi ceremonies, especially those at the Lalish Temple. See "Yezidi Religious Tradition," YezidiTruth.org, accessed December 5, 2018, http://www.yeziditruth.org/yezidi_religious_tradition.

CHAPTER 14: AFTER

To learn more about the Yazidi people and the 2014 genocide, see Yazda's website, https://www.yazda.org. An excellent source and powerful read is the book *The Last Girl: My Story of Captivity, and My Fight Against the Islamic State* by the 2018 Nobel Peace Prize recipient, Nadia Murad (listed in For Further Reading on page 241).

PART V: HOME
CHAPTER 15: EARLY ONE MORNING

p. 173: "Much has been reported about he 1994 massacre of Tutsis by Hutus. . .": For additional information about the Hutus and Tutsis of Burundi, see "Burundi: The situation of the Tutsi, including the Tutsi elite; their treatment by the authorities and by society; and protection provided to them (December 2015–February 2017)," Ref World, UNHCR website, updated January 18, 2019, https://www.refworld.org/docid/58cfb9f14.html.

p. 176: "The name of the camp was Mtendeli . . .": For photographs of Mtendeli refugee camp, search for "Mtendeli Refugee Camp photos."

p. 179: "Probably this compared to the ACT [American College Testing] or SAT [Scholastic Aptitute Test] for high schools here": The ACT and SAT are college entrance exams in the United States. See http://www.act.org or http://collegereadiness.collegeboard.org/sat.

CHAPTER 17: *UMOJA*

The photographs in this chapter were taken during a rehearsal and three church services. The Swahili words and phrases that are included were spoken during the services.

Time Lines

AFGHANISTAN

ca. 500 BCE: Darius of Persia conquers the territory.

ca. 334 BCE: Alexander the Great of Macedonia conquers the territory.

700 CE: Islamic forces conquer the territory.

1218: Genghis Khan conquers the territory.

1400s: Tamerlane conquers the territory.

1839–1842: First Anglo-Afghan war. The British install Shah Shujah as the king. He is assassinated in 1842.

1878–1880: Second Anglo-Afghan war. A treaty gives Britain control of foreign affairs.

1893: Great Britain creates an informal border separating Afghanistan from India.

1919: Emir Amanullah Khan declares Afghanistan an independent country.

1926: Emir Amanullah Khan declares himself king and announces a series of reforms. Three years later, in 1929, civil instability permeates the country. Khan flees. Zahir Shah becomes king, bringing some stability to the country.

1953: The pro-Soviet general Mohammed Daoud, cousin of the king, becomes prime minister and looks to the Soviet Union for economic and military assistance.

1973: Mohammed Daoud overthrows the king in a military coup. He abolishes the monarchy and names himself president. The Republic of Afghanistan is established with strong ties to the USSR.

1978: Mohammed Daoud is killed in a pro-Soviet coup.

1979: The Soviet Union invades Afghanistan. Backed by Soviet troops, Babrak Karmal becomes ruler.

1984: Osama bin Laden of Saudi Arabia travels to Afghanistan to aid anti-Soviet fighters.

1986: The United States supplies the Mujahideen (Afghan rebels) with Stinger missiles, enabling them to shoot down Soviet helicopter gunships.

1989: The Soviets withdraw. Civil war continues.

1992: The Mujahideen fight among themselves for control of Afghanistan.

1996: The Taliban rise to power on promises of peace.

2001: Ignoring international protests, the Taliban destroy ancient Buddhist statues in Bamiyan, Afghanistan, saying they are an affront to Islam.

2001: Hijackers commandeer four commercial airplanes and crash them into the World Trade Center Towers in New York; the Pentagon, outside Washington, D.C.; and a Pennsylvania field. U.S. officials say that Osama bin Laden is the prime suspect in the attack and demand his extradition. The Taliban refuse to turn over bin Laden. U.S. and British forces launch air strikes against targets in Afghanistan.

2002: The Loya Jirga ("grand council") elects U.S.-backed Hamid Karzai as president.

2003: U.S. offensive begins against Kandahar Province and Al-Qaeda. NATO takes command of peacekeeping troops.

2008: U.S. president George W. Bush sends 4,500 additional troops to Afghanistan.

2014: Ashraf Ghani is sworn in as president. NATO, including the U.S. and Great Britain, formally ends its thirteen-year combat operations.

2015: At the request of President Ghani, President Barack Obama delays U.S. troop withdrawal from Afghanistan.

2016: More than 1 million Afghans are displaced during the war. NATO and the U.S. agree to keep troops in place until 2020.

THE KARENS

1824–1826, 1852: The Karens support the British in the first and second Anglo-Burmese wars.

1881: The Karen National Association (KNA) is founded by Western-educated Karens to represent Karen interests with the British.

1885: The Karens support the British in the third Anglo-Burmese war.

1886: Burma becomes a province of British India.

1941–1945: During World War II, the Karens fight alongside Allied forces; the Burmese fight alongside the Japanese.

1948: Great Britain grants Burma independence. Karens and other ethnic populations become incorporated as part of Burma. Massacres in Karen villages quickly follow.

1949: The Karen National Union (KNU), prosperous from imports and logging, uses some of its wealth to arm the Karen National Liberation Army (KNLA).

1960s: "Four Cuts" operations. The Burmese Army targets Karen civilians who support the KNLA.

1962: The Burmese military takes control of the area and turns it into a dictatorship.

1984: The first Karen refugees arrive in Thailand.

1989: The Burmese military changes the name of the country from Burma to Myanmar.

1990s: Karen and other ethnic people move to refugee camps inside the Thai border. The Myanmar army attacks and burns down several camps.

2005: A resettlement program is set up with Western countries.

2011: More than 70,000 Karen people are resettled in the United States.

THE NUERS

1820: Sudan is conquered by Turkey and Egypt. The slave trade develops.

1882: Great Britain invades Sudan.

1885: An Islamic state is founded.

1899: Sudan is governed by British-Egyptian rule.

1955: The First Sudanese Civil War, led by the separatist rebel army Anya-Nya, begins in the North.

1956: Sudan becomes an independent country.

1962: Civil war breaks out in the southern (Christian) part of the country.

1969: Gaafar Nimeiry becomes prime minister of Sudan after a military coup.

1972: The First Sudanese Civil War ends. A peace agreement signed in Addis Ababa, Ethiopia, gives partial autonomy to southern Sudan.

1978: Oil is discovered in Bentiu, in southern Sudan. Sudanese leaders try to redraw the countries' boundaries, transferring the oil fields to the North.

1983: The Second Sudanese Civil War begins. Approximately 26,000 young Nuer and Dinka boys, known as the Lost Boys and Girls of Sudan, are separated from their families.

1985: President Nimeiry is removed from power in a military coup.

2001: Hunger and famine affect 3 million people. The Nile river floods, leaving thousands homeless.

2005: The Second Sudanese Civil War ends.

2005: The North/South Comprehensive Peace Agreement offers a permanent ceasefire and autonomy for the South. Former southern rebel leader John Garang is sworn in as the first vice president but is killed in a plane crash three weeks later.

2011: South Sudan becomes independent and joins the United Nations.

2013: Fighting breaks out between rival ethnic militias, the Nuers and the Dinkas.

2015: A peace agreement between the Dinkas and the Nuers is signed. Smaller ethnic groups are left out. This agreement collapses and fighting resumes.

2017: The U.N. reports on famine caused by civil war and economic collapse. One million children have fled South Sudan. Another million children are displaced within the country. South Sudan becomes the world's fastest-growing refugee crisis.

THE YAZIDIS

637: Muslims burn and destroy much of the Yazidi territory.

980–981: Islamic Kurdish armies massacre Yazidis living in the Hakkar region.

1107: The Muslim expansion massacres about 50,000 Yazidi families.

1218: The Mongols, under the leadership of Hulagu Khan, massacre Yazidi families.

1254: War between Muslims and Yazidis. The Yazidis' sacred shrine at Lalish is desecrated, and the bones of their greatest saint, Sheikh Adi, are taken from his tomb and burned.

1414: Persians, with the help of the Kurds, go to war with the Yazidis.

1585: The Kurds kill more than 600 Yazidis living in Sinjar.

1640–1641: Yazidi villages near Mosul are attacked and looted by the Turkish Ottoman governor.

1715: The army of the Ottoman governor of Baghdad attacks the Yazidis.

1767: Ottoman leader Amin Pasha and his son lead troops against the Yazidis living in Sinjar.

1771: Bedagh Beg, a Yazidi leader, revolts against Amin Pasha. Bedagh Beg is killed along with most of his men.

1785: The Ottoman mayor of Mosul attacks the Yazidis in Sinjar and is at first defeated. He allies with other Arab forces and succeeds.

1795: Ottomans and Kurds destroy Yazidi villages.

1809–1810: The Ottoman mayor of Baghdad attacks the Yazidis in Sinjar.

1838: The Ottoman mayor of Mosul, Tayar Pasha, sends an envoy to the Yazidis with an order to pay taxes. The envoy is killed. Tayar Pasha invades Yazidi villages. The Yazidis withdraw to caves and fight back. Tayar Pasha suffers many loses and returns to Mosul. Peace comes to the Sinjar.

1892: Ottoman leader Omer Wahbi Pasha gives the Yazidis the choice of converting to Islam or paying higher taxes or being killed. Many Yazidis are killed.

1914–1917: During World War I, the Yazidis assist more than 20,000 Armenians fleeing the Ottoman Turks.

1918: The Ottoman air force bombs Sinjar in retribution.

1935: Yazidi leaders revolt against the Iraqi army.

1975: The de facto leader of Iraq, Saddam Hussein, labels the Yazidis "devil worshippers" and begins a new wave of persecution.

2007: The Yazidis stone to death a local girl who wished to convert and marry a Muslim man.

2007: Eight hundred Yazidis are killed when a fuel tanker and three cars filled with explosives are driven into Sinjar villages and detonated.

2014: ISIS (also known as ISIL or the Islamic State) captures Sinjar. Kurdish military troops withdraw without a fight.

HUTUS AND TUTSIS

1300s: Hutu people, believed to have come from the Great Lakes region of West Africa, settle in East Africa.

1400s: Tutsi people, also believed to be from the Great Lakes region of West Africa, settle in East Africa and establish themselves as the rulers.

1500s: The kingdom of Burundi is established.

1890: Kingdoms of Urundi (Burundi) and Ruanda (Rwanda) become part of German East Africa.

1916: The kingdoms of Ruanda and Urundi are conquered by British and Belgian troops during World War I. After the war, they become a Belgian mandate.

1962: As separate nations, Burundi and Rwanda gain independence from Belgium.

1972: The Tutsi-led government in Burundi massacres approximately 100,000 Hutus.

1988: In violent confrontations between the ruling Burundi Tutsis and majority Hutus, more than 150,000 people are killed. Tens of thousands of refugees escape to neighboring countries.

1993: Melchior Ndadaye is elected the first Burundi Hutu president in a democratic election. Five months later, he is assassinated by Tutsi soldiers. In revenge, the Hutu massacre 300,000 Tutsis.

1994: Cyprien Ntaryamira, a Hutu, is appointed president of Burundi by the national assembly. He appoints a Tutsi as his prime minister. President Ntaryamira, along with the president of Rwanda, is killed in a plane crash two months later when they are returning from peace talks. This sets off a wave of massacres between the Hutu and Tutsi.

2004: U.N. forces establish peacekeeping operations in Burundi.

2017: The International Criminal Court begins an investigation into suspected crimes against humanity.

SOURCES

AFGHANISTAN

"Afghanistan Timeline." History Timelines. Accessed December 5, 2018. http://www.datesand events.org/places-timelines/02-afghanistan-timeline.htm.

"History of Afghanistan." History World. Accessed December 5, 2018. http://www.historyworld
.net/wrldhis/PlainTextHistories.asp?historyid=ad09.

THE KARENS

Dwe, Eh Taw, and Tonya Cook. "Karen Refugees from Burma in the US: An Overview for Torture
Treatment Programs." HealTorture.org. Accessed December 5, 2108. https://healtorture
.org/sites/healtorture.org/files/PowerPoint%20Karen%20Refugees%20From%20
Burma%20webinar.pdf.

Falcone, Daniel. "Myanmar and the Karen Conflict: The Longest Civil War You Have Never
Heard Of." Christopher Newman University, Reiff Center blog. January 18, 2016.
http://reiffcenterblog.cnu.edu/2016/01/myanmar-and-the-karen-conflict-the-longest
-civil-war-you-have-never-heard-of.

THE NUERS

"A Brief History of Modern Sudan and South Sudan." Water for South Sudan website. Accessed
December 5, 2018. http://www.waterforsouthsudan.org/brief-history-of-south-sudan.

"South Sudan Profile–Timeline." *BBC News*. August 6, 2018. https://www.bbc.com/news
/world-africa-14019202.

Tchie, Andrew Edward. "Understanding South Sudan's Political Crisis." *The Wire*. May 2, 2017.
https://thewire.in/external-affairs/understanding-south-sudans-political-crisis.

THE YAZIDIS

"History." Yezidis International website. Accessed December 5, 2018. http://www.yezidisinter
national.org/abouttheyezidipeople/history.

"Yezidi Genocide." YezidiTruth.org. Accessed December 5, 2018. http://www.yeziditruth.org
/yezidi_genocide.

HUTUS AND TUTSIS

"Burundi History Timeline." World Atlas. Accessed December 5, 2018. https://www.worldatlas
.com/webimage/countrys/africa/burundi/bitimeln.htm.

"Burundi Profile–Timeline." *BBC News*. December 3, 2018. http://www.bbc.com/news/world
-africa-13087604.

"History of Burundi." History World. Accessed December 5, 2018. http://www.historyworld.net
/wrldhis/PlainTextHistories.asp?historyid=ad25.

Resources

FOR FURTHER READING

Adichie, Chimamanda Ngozi. *Americanah.* New York: Knopf, 2013.

————. *Half of a Yellow Sun.* New York: Knopf, 2006.

Budhos, Marina. *Ask Me No Questions.* New York: Simon and Schuster/Atheneum Books for Young Readers, 2007.

Bulawayo, NoViolet. *We Need New Names.* New York: Little, Brown, 2013.

Cao, Lan. *The Lotus and the Storm.* New York: Penguin, 2014.

Cather, Willa. *My Ántonia.* Boston: Houghton Mifflin, 1918. Reprint, New York: Dover, 1994.

Craig, Charmaine. *Miss Burma.* New York: Grove, 2017.

Gyasi, Yaa. *Homegoing.* New York: Knopf, 2016.

Hamid, Mohsin. *Exit West.* New York: Riverhead, 2017.

Kwok, Jean. *Girl in Translation.* New York: Riverhead, 2010.

Matar, Hisham. *The Return.* New York: Random House, 2016.

Mbue, Imbolo. *Behold the Dreamers.* New York: Random House, 2016.

Minot, Susan. *Thirty Girls.* New York: Knopf, 2014.

Murad, Nadia. *The Last Girl: My Story of Captivity, and My Fight Against the Islamic State.* New York: Tim Duggan, 2017.

Nguyen, Viet Thanh. *The Sympathizer.* New York: Grove, 2015.

Park, Linda Sue. *A Long Walk to Water.* Boston: Clarion, 2010.

Roy, Arundhati. *The Ministry of Upmost Happiness.* New York: Knopf, 2017.

See, Lisa. *The Tea Girl of Hummingbird Lane.* New York: Scribner, 2017.

Yousafzai, Malala. *We Are Displaced: My Journey and Stories from Refugee Girls Around the World.* New York: Little, Brown, 2019.

WEBSITES

To learn more, volunteer, or donate, the following websites are solid places to start. Descriptions are taken from or based on the organizations' mission statements.

American Civil Liberties Union (ACLU)

> "The fundamental constitutional protections of due process and equal protection embodied in our Constitution and Bill of Rights apply to every person, regardless of immigration status. . . . The ACLU Immigrants' Rights Project is dedicated to expanding and enforcing the civil liberties and civil rights of immigrants and to combating public and private discrimination against them." https://www.aclu.org/issues/immigrants-rights

Human Rights Watch

> "Human Rights Watch's Refugee Rights Program defends the rights of refugees, asylum seekers, and displaced people worldwide. We respond to emergencies as well as chronic situations, focusing especially on documenting government efforts to block access to asylum, to deprive asylum seekers of rights to fair hearings of their refugee claims, and to the forcible return of people to places where their lives or freedom would be threatened. We conduct on-the-ground investigations to speak with uprooted people and document abuses against them. We take our findings directly to policy-makers and the media as we advocate for governments to improve access to asylum, to stop forced returns, and to ensure that all migrants are treated with dignity and regard for their basic human rights." https://www.hrw.org/topic/refugee-rights

International Refugee Assistance Project

> The International Refugee Assistance Project "organizes law students and lawyers to develop and enforce a set of legal and human rights for refugees and displaced persons." https://refugeerights.org

International Rescue Committee

> The International Rescue Committee "responds to the world's worst humanitarian crises and helps people whose lives and livelihoods are shattered by conflict and disaster to survive, recover, and regain control of their future." https://www.rescue.org

Lutheran Family Services

> Lutheran Family Services has branches across the U.S. The Nebraska branch's mission is to "express God's love for all people by providing quality human care services that build and strengthen individual, family, and community life." https://www.lfsneb.org

National Immigration Law Center

> NILC is "dedicated to defending and advancing the rights of immigrants with low income." https://www.nilc.org

The Refugee Law Reader

> The Refugee Law Reader: Cases, Documents and Materials is a comprehensive online model curriculum for the study of the complex and rapidly evolving field of international refugee law, covering Africa, the Americas, Asia, and Europe. The Reader is for professors, lawyers, advocates, and students across a wide range of national jurisdictions. www.refugeelawreader.org/en/about-the-reader.html

United Nations High Commissioner for Refugees

> "UNHCR, the U.N. Refugee Agency, is a global organization dedicated to saving lives, protecting rights and building a better future for refugees, forcibly displaced communities, and stateless people." http://www.unhcr.org

World Food Program

> "WFP is the leading humanitarian organization fighting hunger worldwide, delivering food assistance in emergencies and working with communities to improve nutrition and build resilience. As the international community has committed to end hunger, achieve food security and improved nutrition by 2030, one in nine people worldwide still do not have enough to eat. Food and food-related assistance lie at the heart of the struggle to break the cycle of hunger and poverty." http://www1.wfp.org

Yazda Global Organization

> Yazda is a multinational association that began after the Yazidi Genocide in 2014. Yazda's goal is to "build a stronger Yazidi community that can socially and culturally integrate into the U.S. and to preserve the Yazidi culture at the same time." https://www.yazda.org

Index

Page numbers in italics indicate maps, images, and/or captions.